SOCIAL CHANGE IN WESTERN EUROPE

MUSLIMS IN EUROPE

edited by
BERNARD LEWIS
and
DOMINIQUE SCHNAPPER

PINTER
PUBLISHERS
LONDON, NEW YORK

DISTRIBUTED IN THE USA AND CANADA BY ST MARTIN'S PRESS INC

Pinter Publishers
25 Floral Street, Covent Garden, London, WC2E 9DS, United Kingdom

First published in Great Britain in 1994

Distributed Exclusively in the USA and Canada by St Martin's Press, Inc., Room 400, 175 Fifth Avenue, New York, NY10010, USA

British Library Cataloguing in Publication Data
A CIP catalogue record for this book is available from The British Library

ISBN 1 85567 250 2 (hb)
    1 85567 214 6 (pb)

Library of Congress Cataloging-in-Publication Data

Muslims in Europe / edited by Bernard Lewis and Dominique Schnapper.
        p. cm. – (Social change in Western Europe)
    Includes bibliographical references and index.
    ISBN 1–85567–250–2. – ISBN 1–85567–214–6 (pbk.)
    1. Muslims–Europe–History. 2. Europe–Ethnic relations. 3. Social change. I. Lewis, Bernard. II. Schnapper, Dominique. III. Series.
    D1056.2.M87M86 1994
    940'.0882971-dc20   94–17103
                                                                                            CIP

Typeset by Saxon Graphics Ltd, Derby
Printed and bound in Great Britain

SOCIAL CHANGE IN WESTERN EUROPE

MUSLIMS IN EUROPE

The *Social Change in Western Europe* series developed from the need to provide a summary of current thinking from leading academic thinkers on major social and economic issues concerning the evolving policies of Western Europe in the post-Maastricht era. To create an effective European Union governments and politicians throughout the region must work to provide satisfactory social, economic and political conditions for the populations of Europe, and each volume affords an opportunity to look at specific issues and their impact on individual countries.

The series is directed by an academic committee composed of Arnaldo Bagnasco (Turin University), Henri Mendras (CNRS, Paris) and Vincent Wright (Nuffield, Oxford), assisted by Patrick Le Galès (CNRS, Rennes), Anand Menon (University of Oxford) with the support of Michel Roger and Oliver Cazenave (Futuroscope in Poitiers). This group forms the *Observatoire du Changement en Europe Occidentale* which was launched in Poitiers (France) in 1990 with the generous funding of the Fondation de Poitiers headed by Renè Monory.

SOCIAL CHANGE IN WESTERN EUROPE

IN THE SAME SERIES

The Return to Incomes Policy
edited by R.P.DORE, ROBERT BOYER & ZOE MARS

Long-Term Unemployment
edited by D'ODILE BENOIT-GUILBOT & DUNCAN GALLIE

The Ethics of Medical Choice
edited by JON ELSTER & NICOLAS HERPIN

Youth in Europe
edited by ALESSANDRO CAVALLI & OLIVER GALLAND

Small-and Medium-Size Enterprises
edited by ARNALDO BAGNASCO & HENRI MENDRAS

CONTENTS

LIST OF CONTRIBUTORS

Han Entzinger is Professor of Multi-ethnic studies at the Unversity of Utrecht and Academic Director of the European Centre for Research on Migration and Interethnic Relations (ERCOMER) at the same university.

Friedrich Heckmann is Professor of Sociology at the University of Bamberg and he chairs the 'Migration and Ethnic Minorities' group in the German Sociology Association. He has published *Die Bundesrepublik: ein Einwanderungsland?* (Stuttgart, Klett-Cotta, 1981); *Ethnische Minderheiten, Volk und Nation, Soziologie interethnischer Beziehungen* (Stuttgart, Enke Verlag, 1992).

Charles Husband is Professor of Social Analysis at the University of Bradford. He has published *'Race' in Britain, Continuity and Change* (London Hutchinson, 1987, 2 ed.).

Johannes, J.G. Jansen is an Islamologist and former Director of the Netherlands Institute for Egyptian Archaeology and Arabic Studies in Cairo. He is a professor at the University of Leiden. Among his publications are *The Interpretation of the Koran in Modern Egypt* (Leiden, Brill, 1980) and *Inleiding tot de Islam* (Muiteberg, Coutinho, 1987).

Bernard Lewis is Emeritus Professor of Near Eastern Studies at Princeton University. He has published numerous works of reference on Islam that have been translated into many languages. His latest book *Race and Slavery in Islam: an historical inquiry* was published by the Oxford University Press in 1990.

Bernhard Nauck is Professor of Sociology at the Pädagogischen Hochschule in Weingarten. He has published 'Assimilation process and group integration of migrant families', *International*

Migration, 27: 27–48, 1989; and 'Intergenerational Relationships in Families from Turkey in Germany, an extension of the 'value children' approach to educational attitudes and socialisation practices', *European Sociological Review*, 5: 251–274, 1989.

Nadia Rachedi teaches at the University of Paris VIII (Saint-Denis) and is completing her doctorate at the Ecole des Hautes Etudes - Sciences Sociales (EHESS)

Olivier Roy holds a research appointment at the CNRS and is a member of the group Sciences sociales du monde iranien contemporain'.

Dominique Schnapper is Director of Studies at the Ecole des Hautes Etudes - Sciences Sociales (EHESS). She has published *La France de l'intègration,* (Paris, Gillimard, 1991) and *L'Europe des immigrès, essai sur les politiques d'immigration,* (Paris, François Bourin, 1992).

Pnina Werbner is engaged in research at the University of Manchester. She has published *The Migration Process: capital, gifts and offerings among British Pakistanis* (Oxford, Berg Publishers, 1990); and with M. Anwar, edited *Black and Ethnic Leaderships in Britain, the cultural dimension of political action,* (London, Routledge, 1991).

1

LEGAL AND HISTORICAL REFLECTIONS ON THE POSITION OF MUSLIM POPULATIONS UNDER NON-MUSLIM RULE

BERNARD LEWIS

One of the earliest Muslim visitors to Western Europe in modern times was a certain Mīrzā Abū Tālib Khān, an Indian of Perso-Turkish background, who travelled in England and France between 1798 and 1803, and wrote an extensive and detailed account of his travels, adventures and impressions. During his stay in London he was taken several times to the Houses of Parliament. He was not impressed by what he saw, remarking that the oratory reminded him of the squawking of a flock of parrots. However, he was astonished when he found that this was a legislative assembly, with the duty of enacting laws to regulate both civil and criminal matters – defining offences and prescribing penalties. The English, he explained to his readers, unlike the Muslims, did not accept any divinely revealed holy law to guide them and regulate their lives in these matters and were therefore reduced to the pitiable expedient of making their own laws 'in accordance with the exigencies of the time, their own dispositions, and the experience of their judges'.

In this comment, Mīrzā Abū Ṭālib Khān was revealing an essential difference between classical Islamic and modern Western views on the nature of law and authority, and therefore of the functions and jurisdiction of the state. For the Muslim, law is an essential, indeed a central part of his religion, which is inconceivable without it. The law in all its details is divine not human, revealed not enacted, and cannot therefore be repealed or abrogated, supplemented or amended. Deriving from the same authority and sustained by the same sanctions, it deals equally with what we would call public and private, civil and criminal, ritual and even dietary matters. Its jurisdiction is in principle universal, since God's revelation is for all mankind, but in practice personal and communal, since its enforcement is limited to those who accept it and submit to its authority. For such, its authority is absolute and applies to every aspect of human life and activity. In theory, therefore, there is no legislative power in human society, since the making of laws is for God alone. According to a frequently cited Muslim dictum, to forbid what God permits is no less an offence than to permit what God forbids. This principle is of obvious relevance to certain contemporary situations in which modern social mores conflict with traditional Islamic practice.

While in principle there is no legislative function in the Islamic state, in practice Muslim rulers and jurists, during the fourteen centuries that have elapsed since the life of the Prophet, have encountered many problems for which revelation provided no explicit answers, and have found answers to them. These answers were never seen as enactments nor presented as legislation. If they came from below, they were called custom. If they came from government, they were called regulation. If they came from the jurists, they were called interpretation. Like lawyers everywhere, Muslim religious lawyers could accomplish many changes by the reinterpretation of even the most sacrosanct texts.

For Muslims, the most sacred text – indeed the only text to which that adjective can properly be applied – is the Qur'ān. The Qur'ān is the primary source of holy law and where it contains a clear and unequivocal statement, this is accepted as an eternal commandment equally valid for all times and all places. The clearer and more explicit the statement, the less room there is for interpretation. But where, as often, the statement is elliptic or allusive, there is a need for interpretation and an opportunity for creative ingenuity.

The scope for interpretative ingenuity is correspondingly greater in dealing with the second major source of Islamic law, the corpus of traditions, transmitted through the generations, describing the actions and utterances of the Prophet. Such traditions are known as *hadīth*. While *hadīth* is also binding and in principle equally so, it differs from the Qur'ān in an important practical respect. While there is a single Qur'ān with an undisputed text, there are vast numbers of different and sometimes contradictory *hadīths*, some of them surviving in variant versions and many of them regarded as questionable or even false by respected authorities. The collection, transmission, study and authentication of such traditions became a major branch of Muslim religious scholarship. In time scholars assembled a considerable body of traditions, which were widely accepted among Muslims as authentic. But even these were subject to a variety of interpretations, often differing considerably. To regulate this, certain principles of interpretation were accepted, involving analogy and other forms of reasoning and even, within limits, the exercise of independent judgement. The dominant principle accepted by the vast majority of Muslims was the *sunna*, a word meaning practice or precedent, and specialized to mean the practice of the Prophet and his Companions and other revered early Muslims, sanctified by tradition. According to a much cited saying attributed to the Prophet, 'my community will not agree upon an error'. This was interpreted as meaning that after the death of the Prophet, God's guidance passed to the Muslim community as a whole, and has led to the acceptance of the doctrine of consensus, in Arabic *ijmā'*, which might be approximately translated as the climate of opinion among the powerful, the learned and the pious. To follow precedent was *sunna*, and considered to be good. Departure from precedent was *bid'a*, innovation – the nearest Muslim equivalent to the Christian notion of heresy.

The principle of consensus made it possible for jurists over a period of time, in one or other part of the Muslim world, in practice though never in theory, to modify and adapt the law to meet changing circumstances. They were further helped in this by another principle laid down by the jurists, that of *darūra* necessity. Even in the Qur'ān there are verses that permit, sometimes implicitly and sometimes even explicitly, on ground of necessity, what would otherwise be forbidden. As developed by the jurists, the principle of necessity applied in two forms. The first, relating to individuals, deals with the dire constraints under which a person might find himself. A Muslim may for example eat pork or carrion rather than starve to death. A seafarer may throw another seafarer's goods into the sea if their boat is overladen and about to sink. In the second sense, necessity no longer refers to individual constraint, but rather to the exigencies of social and economic – and some would add political – life. But the principle of *darūra* has limits. For the individual, these are clear and unequivocal. Thus, for example, a Muslim may eat pork to save his life, but he may not commit murder. The social limits are more subtle, more debated, and, of course, more relevant.

The most important among those who rejected the Sunnī view are the Shī'atu 'Alī, the faction or party of 'Alī, the major break-away group in Islam. In the classical Sunnī perception, the Muslim community is guided by God, its ruler is ordained and approved by God, and its history reveals the working out of God's purpose for mankind. For the Shī'a, all the sovereigns of Islam since the abdica-tion of Hasan, the son of 'Alī, the founder of their sect, in the year 41 of the *hijra*, are usurpers. The Muslim world is living in sin and history has taken a wrong turning. In practice, the two differed rather less from each other than their doctrines would appear to require. The Shī'a found themselves obliged to make a series of compromises and live at peace under rulers whom theoretically they regarded as tyrants and usurpers. Sunnīs for their part were obliged to compromise on their definitions of what constitutes a legitimate and just ruler, and to accept a series of usurpers and tyrants, whose only claim to power was the possession of sufficient military force to seize and hold it. Accepting them meant recogniz-ing their legitimacy in terms of *sharī'a*, and this in turn meant that obedience to them was a religious obligation, disobedience a sin as well as a crime. Tyranny, according to a common saying, is better than anarchy. The reason was eloquently set forth by the eleventh-century theologian and philosopher Ghazālī:

Which is better, to declare that the qāḍis are revoked, that all authoriza-tions are invalid, that marriages cannot be legally contracted, that all acts of government everywhere are null and void and thus to allow that the entire population is living in sin – or is it better to recognize that the imamate exists in fact and therefore that transactions and administrative actions are valid, given the actual circumstances and the necessities of these times?

Other scholars go even further and say that any ruler who can seize power and maintain order – even if he is barbarous or vicious – must be recognized and obeyed 'for the welfare of the Muslims and the preservation of their unity (i.e. their social cohesion)'. From a barbarian and a tyrant to an infidel it was only one step, but a very difficult one. Some writers were willing to take even that step, and from the eleventh century we find Arabic and Persian authors quoting a maxim, and sometimes even, absurdly, attribut-ing it to the Prophet, that a just infidel is preferable to an unjust Muslim ruler – or, as some put it, government can exist with unbe-lief, but not with injustice. The more usual view among the jurists, for whom justice is defined by the holy law of Islam, is that the worst of Muslims is preferable to the best of infidels.

In the course of time, different schools of jurisprudence arose among the Muslims. The Shī'a, of course, have their own, but even among the Sunnīs several different schools emerged in the Middle Ages, four of which have survived to the present time. These are the Mālikī school, which predominates in almost the whole of Muslim Africa outside Egypt; the Shāfi'ī school, which is found principally in the Eastern Arab countries and among the Muslims of South and Southeast Asia; the Hanafī school, in Turkey, Central Asia, and the Indian sub-continent; and the Hanbalī school, in Saudi Arabia. While these differ from each other on many minor and a few major points, all nevertheless recognize each other as Muslim and within the limits of permitted difference of opinion. Indeed there is a tradition, almost certainly spurious, according to which the Prophet said: 'Difference of opinion within my community is a sign of God's mercy.'

In most systems of law, actions are divided into two categories, permitted and forbidden, or, in religious matters, commanded and forbidden. Islamic law, dealing with both religious and worldly matters, divides actions into five categories, which one might render as:

1. required, commanded;
2. recommended;
3. permitted;
4. disapproved;
5. forbidden.

The first category is subdivided into individual and collective commandments. Thus, for example, the duty of fighting in *jihād*, the holy war for Islam, is a collective duty on the community as a whole in offence, but becomes an individual duty of every able-bodied male Muslim in defence.

It is under the heading of *jihād* that the Muslim jurists normally discuss the various legal problems arising from relations between Muslims and non-Muslims – authorities, communities, individuals. The reason for this classification is clear. Muslims, like Christians, believe that the revelation which has been given to them is for all mankind, and that it is their sacred duty to bring it to those who are not aware of it or have not yet accepted it. In the language of the holy law this obligation is known as *jihād*, usually translated as holy war but literally meaning striving. In later times this was sometimes interpreted in a moral sense. In classical juristic literature it is invariably interpreted in a military sense and the jurists go into great detail on such questions as the opening, conduct, and termination of hostilities, the treatment of prisoners and non-combatants, the definition and division of booty.

Islamic teaching and, with few exceptions, Islamic practice reject forcible conversion. However, the power of the Islamic state and therefore the jurisdiction of Islamic law were extended in the early centuries of the Islamic era over vast territories and population. The literature of the time clearly reflects the belief that this process would continue without interruption until, in a not too distant future, the whole world either accepted the Islamic faith or submitted to Muslim rule. In the meantime, the world was divided into two, the *Dār al-Islām*, the House of Islam, in which Islamic government and Islamic law prevailed, and the *Dār al-Harb*, the House of War, where infidel rulers still remained in power. The denizens of the *Dār al- Harb* were known as *harbī*.

The swift vast conquests achieved by the early Muslims brought great numbers of non-Muslims into the Islamic empire; for some time they constituted the majority of the population. Even after their majority status was ended by conversion and assimilation, they remained in significant numbers as minoritics living among the now Muslim majority. Later, when the first great wave of conquest was finished and a more or less stable frontier was established between the House of Islam and the House of War, other non-Muslims came to the Islamic lands as visitors or as temporary residents, sometimes as students or diplomats, most commonly for purposes of trade. Muslim law deals at some length and in great detail with the first group and also devotes some attention to the second.

Non-Muslims who were permitted to live as permanent residents under Muslim rule were called *dhimm ī*, that is to say members of a community which had been granted a *dhimma* a pact, by the Muslim authorities. Under the terms of the *dhimma* the non-Muslim subjects agreed to recognize the primacy of Islam and the supremacy of the Muslims. Their submission was symbolized by the payment of a poll tax and the acceptance of certain social restrictions, notably proscription to bear arms. In return, they were allowed to practice their religion, to maintain and when necessary repair their places of worship (a ban on the construction of new churches and synagogues was rarely enforced). In general they enjoyed a large degree of autonomy under their own religious chiefs, to whom they owed obedience, and who exercised jurisdiction over them. Apart from the measures necessary to protect the security of the state, maintain public order and decency, and safeguard the primacy of Islam, they lived by their own and not by Muslim law. Most civil matters, including marriage, divorce and inheritance, as well as disputes between members of the same community, were heard before their own courts and decided by their own judges according to their own laws. Education was also the responsibility of their community chiefs, who controlled schools, teachers and curricula.

The visitor or temporary resident from abroad was called *musta' min* the holder of an *amān*, or safe conduct. This might be personal or might be granted to the country of which the visitor was a subject. The *musta'min* was exempt from the poll tax and many of the other restrictions imposed on the *dhimmī*, but enjoyed the same right to live by his own laws and under his own ruler, in this case usually the consul of his city or country. The *amān* was normally granted for a limited time and could be renewed. If the *musta'min* overstayed his *amān*, he became a *dhimmī*. The foreign communities, under the authority of their consuls, functioned as autonomous states within the state. In later centuries, when the changing balance of military and economic power transformed the relationship between the West and the Islamic world, what had originally been a voluntary concession granted by Muslim governments in accordance with the logic of their own laws became a ruthlessly enforced and bitterly resented extra-territorial privilege imposed by the now dominant Western powers.

In the early centuries of Islam, when the juristic schools were formed and the major legal treatises were written, the status of temporary or permanent non-Muslims under Muslim rule was a current and almost universal issue, and therefore needed elaborate consideration and regulation. The corresponding problem of Muslims under non-Muslim rule hardly arose, and where it did, received only minor and fleeting attention. In an age when the frontiers of Islam were continually expanding and when such losses of territory as occurred were tactical and temporary, it was hardly likely that the jurists would devote much attention to what was largely a hypothetical question.

When this question is discussed at all it is, naturally enough, under the same general heading *jihād*, and in the same categories (permanent resident and temporary visitor) as the status of the non-Muslim under Muslim rule. In the earliest juristic literature, the position of a Muslim permanently resident in a non-Muslim land is considered only in one contingency, that of an infidel in the land of the infidels who sees the light and embraces Islam – surely a rare occurrence. The question they discuss is whether he may remain where he is or must leave his home and migrate to a Muslim country. The Shī'a jurists, more attuned to the idea of surviving in a hostile environment and under a hostile authority, allow him to stay and indeed see him as an outpost and beacon of Islam. The majority of Sunnī jurists, accustomed to the association of religion and authority, insist that he must leave and remove himself to a Muslim land where he can live in accordance with the holy law of Islam. In this he would be following the sacred precedent set by the Prophet and his Companions when they left their homes in pagan.Mecca and undertook the migration (hijra) to Medina, where they established the first Muslim state and community. Some jurists even go so far as to say that if he remains where he is and his country is subsequently conquered by the Muslims, then his non-Muslim family and his property are liable to be treated as booty by the conquerors in the same way as those of his infidel neighbors and compatriots.

Two cases of such conversion cited in the biographies of the Prophet indicate that the departure of a convert would be an act of expediency as well as of piety. The Byzantine governor of Ma'ān in South Jordan embraced Islam and wrote to the Prophet. When he refused to recant he was executed by the Byzantine authorities. Another story tells of a churchman at the court of Byzantium who responded to the Prophet's summons and publicly recited the Muslim profession of faith, whereupon he was beaten to death by the crowd.

The question of a Muslim traveller to the lands of the infidels for a voluntary or involuntary, brief or protracted visit was of more practical concern and receives more attention. Prisoners captured in war or at sea had no choice, and the jurists offer guidelines on how a Muslim who suffers this misfortune should conduct himself, until he is ransomed, exchanged, or escapes. As regards voluntary visitors, the first question to be decided was whether such visits are permissible at all in law and, if so, under what circumstances and subject to what rules. Mālik, the founder of the Mālikī school, allows Muslims to visit the lands of the infidels for one purpose only – to ransom captives. It is significant that the reports of the Moroccan ambassadors to the various courts of Europe are almost all headed 'Report of a Mission for the Ransoming of Captives', no doubt in order to avoid possible legal difficulties for themselves or for their sovereign.

There was lively discussion among Mālikī jurists as to whether it was permissible to travel to the lands of the infidels for purposes of trade and specifically in order to buy foodstuffs during periods of dearth in the lands of Islam. Juristic answers to this question fall into three main groups. According to one group, it is forbidden in all circumstances to trade with the infidel, since they would use their profits to make war against Islam. If this means famine, then it must be endured. A second group, invoking the principle of *darūra*, necessity, allow trade and travel only in order to secure supplies of foodstuffs in times of shortage. A third group are more willing to extend a general tolerance to Muslim travel and temporary residence abroad, and allow a Muslim to accept *amān* from a non-Muslim government and stay for a while in a non-Muslim country, with the status of *musta'min*. The assumption is that he would enjoy the same privileges and accept the same duties as applied to an infidel *musta'min* in a Muslim land. The acceptance by a Muslim of a non-Muslim *amān* is subject to certain conditions from the Muslim side, the most important of which is that he be able to 'manifest the signs of Islam'. This phrase, which occurs frequently in discussions of Muslims *in partibus*, will need some further consideration.

The presence of Muslims, in groups or even as individuals, in the House of War raised the question of jurisdiction, to which the juristic schools give different answers. Are such Muslims still subject to Muslim law? Of more practical importance, are Muslim judges empowered to deal with persons living, or actions committed, under infidel rule? The Shī'a say yes, the Hanafīs usually say no, and the others adopt a variety of intermediate positions.

Muslim discussions of these matters were concerned almost exclusively with Christendom, seen as the House of War *par excellence*. The jurists were much less worried about the colonies of Muslim merchants established from early times in India, China and other parts of Asia and Africa. These were, so to speak, religiously neutral zones, offering no threat to Islam in either the religious or the political sense. On the contrary, their peoples were seen as potential recruits to the Islamic faith and their lands as potential additions to the Islamic domains. This expectation proved historically justified. Only in Christendom did Muslims encounter a rival and in many respects a similar religio-political power, challenging their claim both to universal truth and to universal authority.

The first recorded agreement between the Muslim state and a Christian state was with the Christian kingdom of Nubia, to the south of Egypt. Modern critical scholarship has cast doubt on both the modalities and the chronology of this agreement as reported by the chroniclers, but from the point of view of the jurists what matters is not the reconstituted reality but the traditional narrative. According to this, in the year 31 of the *hijra*, corresponding to 652 of the common era, a pact was concluded with the king of Nubia stipulating, among other things, that the king would:

protect those Muslims ... who tarry or travel there until they leave ... maintain the mosque that the Muslims have built in the centre of [his] city and not hinder anyone from praying there ... and keep it swept, lit and treated with respect.

The Nubian pact served as starting point for some later juridical theories and arrangements, whereby certain territories were regarded as falling into an intermediate category between the House of Islam and the House of War, variously designated a *Dār al-Sulḥ*, the House of Truce, or *Dār al-'Ahd*, the House of Pact or Covenant. Such arrangements existed both in medieval and in Ottoman times, and the countries in question were usually in a tributary or subordinate relationship to the Islamic state. Agreement with these states normally provided for Muslim travel and even residence in their territories, with virtually extra-territorial privileges. No such arrangement was possible with Christian states, which remained fully independent and were therefore presumed hostile.

The tenth century saw the beginning of a Christian recovery and counterattack, which in time forced the retreat, sometimes temporary, sometimes permanent, of the Muslims from many of the former Christian territories that they had conquered and dominated. Already in the tenth century, a Byzantine advance brought much of northern Syria back under Christian rule. In the eleventh century the Norman Conquest recovered Sicily for Christendom and shortly after the Crusaders established four Christian principalities in the Levant, between Taurus and Sinai, in lands which had been held by Islam since the seventh century. Most important of all, the long struggle for the reconquest of the Iberian peninsula gained significant victories in the eleventh and succeeding centuries, and was finally completed with the fall of Granada, the last Muslim principality in Western Europe, in 1492.

Even greater disasters struck the Muslims in the East, when the great Mongol conquests of the thirteenth century brought central Asia, Iran and Iraq under pagan rule, and for a while seemed to threaten Syria and even Egypt. Muslim historians did not fail to note that there were Christians among the Mongols, and that these seemed to enjoy some favour. They tell in particular of a dramatic incident in 1260 when the Mongol forces entered the city of Damascus. Their commander was a Nestorian Christian from the East, and he rode through the city flanked by two other Christian princes, one an Armenian, the other a Crusader.

With the decline of Muslim power and the rise of modern Europe, the problem was compounded, as province after province, country after country, was conquered and annexed to the great European empires – first Austria and Russia, then the maritime powers of Western Europe. All these Christian advances brought large Muslim populations under Christian rule and confronted them with a new and agonizing problem.

The problem, as usually formulated in the juridical literature, is as follows: 'If their country has been conquered by the Christians, may Muslims stay or must they migrate to a Muslim land?'

The term that they use – migration, in Arabic *hijra* – indicates how the problem is seen in terms of Islamic jurisprudence. According to Muslim teaching, the Prophet was a model (the Arabic phrase is *uswa hasana*) to be followed by the Muslims in almost all respects. The Prophet himself had set the example of migration by leaving pagan Mecca and enjoining his followers to accompany or precede him in the migration to Medina, where they would be able to live a Muslim life. The obligation of Muslims to migrate to a place where they can practice their religion freely is based on a passage in the Qur'ān (IV, 97–100) supported by a number of *hadith*s. In a characteristic and frequently cited saying, the Prophet denounces and rejects any Muslim who chooses to live among the polytheists.

In the early centuries of Islam, the question of *hijra* was purely theoretical and some jurists, notably of the Hanafī school, argued that the obligation of *hijra* ceased to operate after the Muslim conquest of Mecca. They even adduce a *hadith* to this effect: 'There is no *hijra* after the conquest [of Mecca].' The tide of Christian reconquest gave the question a new relevance and urgency, and the Mālikī jurists of the West, confronted by the subjugation of extensive Muslim territories in Sicily, Spain and Portugal, gave a different answer. The obligation of *hijra*, they declared, has not lapsed but will remain in effect until the Day of Judgement. The only questions are when and in what circumstances it applies, and when and for whom it may be remitted.

Some jurists find authority in the Qur'ān and in *ḥadīth*s for exemption on ground of physical or financial incapacity. Some invoke the principle of *darūra*, necessity, both personal and communal, to allow significant postponements of the inevitable departure. Others allow Muslims to stay in the hope of 'guiding the people of unbelief to the truth and saving them from error'. But all agree that it is a bad thing for Muslims to remain under non-Muslim rule, the principal disagreement being whether such an action falls under the heading of disapproved or forbidden or, to put it another way, whether emigration is commanded or merely recommended. The key question is whether they are permitted to practice their religion or, more precisely, to 'manifest the signs of Islam'. If they are not, then all agree that they must leave. If they are, then the moderates see their continued presence as disapproved, while the more rigorous jurists insist that even then they are bound by religious law to leave. The Moroccan jurist Aḥmad al-Wansharīsī, writing in the final stages of the Christian reconquest of Spain, insists that even if the Christian conquerors are both just and tolerant, the Muslims are still required to leave – indeed, even more so, since under such a regime the danger of apostasy would be correspondingly greater.

In their particular case, the question was entirely hypothetical, since the Christian conquerors were neither just nor tolerant, and the Muslims were obliged to leave irrespective of their own choice or preference. Other Muslims conquered by Christian European powers were more fortunate, and the choice whether to stay or to go remained their own. Into modern times the term *muhājir*, one who performs *hijra*, has been used of Muslims who migrated from the lost provinces of the Ottoman Empire to Turkey, and from secular India to Pakistan.

The choice they made, and the juridical ratification of their choice, depended very largely on how far they were free to practice their religion and how in fact that freedom was understood by them. For the modern Westerner, religious freedom is defined by the phrase 'freedom of worship', and means just that. But the practice of Islam means more than worship, important as that may be. It means a whole way of life, prescribed in detail by the holy texts and treatises based on them. Nor is that all. The primary duty of the Muslim as set down not once but many times in the Qur'ān is to command good and forbid evil'. It is not enough to do good and refrain from evil as a personal choice. It is incumbent upon Muslims also to command and forbid – that is to exercise authority. The same principle applied in general to the holy law, which must not only be obeyed but also enforced. Thus, in the view of many jurists, a Muslim must not only abstain from drinking and dissipation; he must also destroy strong drink and other appurtenances of dissipation. For this reason, in any encounter between Islam and unbelief, Islam must dominate. That is why mosques must overtop non-Muslim places of worship and never be overtopped by them and why – on this point the jurists are unanimous – a Muslim man may marry a non-Muslim woman, but a non-Muslim man may not, on pain of death, marry a Muslim woman. In marriage, so the jurists believed, the husband is always the dominant partner.

A similar asymmetry appears in the law concerning proselytizing. It is the duty of a Muslim, wherever he may be, to bring the faith to the unbelievers. Islam, unlike Christianity, has no professional missionaries, but assigns this task to all Muslims alike. It is however strictly forbidden for a *dhimmī* to try to convert a Muslim to his religion, and if by any mischance he succeeds, the penalty for apostasy is death. From a Muslim religious point of view, this discrepancy is both logical and proper. To promote the true faith is a divine commandment. To abandon it, or to persuade another to do so, is both a mortal sin and a capital crime.

There are some who follow this argument to its logical conclusion and maintain that an authentic Muslim life is only possible under a Muslim government. There are others who reject this extremist view and admit the possibility of living a Muslim life under a non-Muslim government, provided that that government meets certain specific requirements. The Hanafi school, in this as in most other matters inclined to moderate positions, was satisfied with basic tolerance and imposed migration only when Muslims suffered forced conversion or were prevented from performing their religious duties. Even then, emigration was only obligatory for those who had the necessary means. The Mālikī school, as well as other Eastern schools, was more rigorous, and regarded emigration as being at the very least recommended and in most cases obligatory

The criterion in deciding whether residence in their homeland is forbidden or merely disapproved of is the application of Muslim holy law. If the affairs of the Muslims are conducted in accordance with the holy law, and are adjudicated by Muslim *qādī*s in courts administering that law, then according to some of the jurists they may remain, and the actions of such *qādīs*, even if they are appointed by infidel authorities, are valid. For a significant number of jurists, remaining where one is in such circumstances is disapproved of but not forbidden. For the most rigorous, even in the most favorable circumstances Muslims are forbidden to stay and are required to leave.

Nevertheless, in spite of these strictures, many did stay, and during the centuries of the *Reconquista* in Spain there were times when considerable Muslim populations lived under the newly-established Christian governments, to whom they paid tribute in return for tolerance. They were despised by both the emigrants and the unconquered, who saw them as *dhimmī*s of the Christians. They were known by the Arabic terms *ahl al-dajn* or *mudajjan*, a word used to denote tame or domesticated as contrasted with wild and free animals. The word passed into Spanish in the form *mudejar*. The steady worsening of the condition of the *mudejar* subjects of the Christian states gave added strength to the rigorist point of view, and a series of *fatwā*s by Andalusian and North African jurists reiterated that it was the duty of the Muslims of Spain to leave their conquered homelands and seek refuge under the rule of Islam. No less a person than Ibn Rushd, *qādī* and *imām* of the great mosque of Cordova and grandfather of the philosopher known in Europe as Averroes, laid down that the duty of *hijra* is eternal. A Muslim must not remain where he is subject to the jurisdiction of the polytheists, but must leave and go to the lands of the Muslims, where he will be subject to Muslim jurisdiction. Just as the Companions of the Prophet were permitted to return to Mecca after it was conquered, so the *muhājir* will be permitted to return to his homeland when it is restored to Islam.

The dilemma of the Muslim populations of Iberia and Sicily was resolved by their voluntary or enforced departure. Centuries later the Muslim populations of the lost Tatar and Turkish lands in Europe had a freer choice. Many left voluntarily; others remained to endure a difficult existence as a minority in Russia and in the newly independent Christian states. The dilemma arose in a more acute form with the establishment of European imperial rule in countries of predominantly Muslim population – the French in North Africa, the Russians in the Black Sea and Caspian regions and in Central Asia, the British and the Dutch in South and Southeast Asia. At first some Muslim leaders and jurists applied the rule of emigration even in these places, and significant numbers to Muslims went from North Africa to Turkey, from the Russian Empire to Turkey and Iran, from India to Afghanistan. But the vast majority perforce remained, and they and their leaders and teachers had to adapt themselves to a new reality. With the exception of the state-imposed secularism and atheism of the Soviet era, the imperial regimes in general were, for good reasons of their own, tolerant of religious matters. They allowed Muslims not only the free practice of their religion in the limited Western sense of that word, but also the maintenance and enforcement of their own laws, through their own judges and courts, over a wide range of social, personal and even some economic matters. Muslim jurists responded to this and some were even willing to rule that a country where Muslims live and where Muslim law is enforced may be considered part of the House of Islam, even if the sovereign authority is in the hands of infidels. Others, while not prepared to go that far, accepted a variety of compromises, mostly justified by necessity, *darūra*.

In the last analysis, the real test of whether Muslims may stay or go is the holy law by which they must live. The primary concern of the classical jurists was to maintain that law. The main aim of the modern fundamentalists is to restore it where it has been neglected or set aside. For some, including most of the Mālikī school, no place conquered by infidels can be considered under Muslim law, and Muslims must sooner or later leave, when they have the means and the capacity. For others, the mere fact of conquest by infidels does not make a country part of the House of War. If the holy law is still maintained and enforced, even under infidel authority, that country may still be considered, for legal purposes, as part of the House of Islam. Jurists are in particular concerned with the validity of legal actions and documents, and the legitimacy of the *qāḍis* who validate them. They give primary importance to the laws relating to marriage and divorce, and to inheritance and other matters of property. Without the one, Muslims may find that they are living in sin; without the other, they cannot be sure of the lawful enjoyment of their worldly goods.

The colonial empires had allowed this type of communal legal autonomy to the Muslims living under their rule. Before that, Muslim rulers from the first Arab caliphs to the last Ottoman sultans had allowed the Christian communities to live by their own laws of personal status and to provide for their own schooling and higher education. To many Muslims it seemed reasonable to expect the same courtesy from the governments of their new homes abroad. In fact they received far more personal freedom, but far less communal autonomy than had been accorded to the Christian subjects of Muslim states.

The resulting dilemma is epitomized in the no doubt apocryphal complaint of a recent Muslim immigrant to Europe: 'We allowed Christians to practice and even enforce monogamy under Muslim rule, so why shouldn't you allow us to practice polygamy under Christian rule?' The difficulty arises not only from conflicting social mores, as in this and similar cases, but also, more especially, from an understanding of identity and jurisdiction that is clearly out of accord with the accepted practice of most of the modern world, including some of the Muslim states. In Turkey the *shari'a* law was legally abolished, but was unofficially maintained in remote rural areas. As a result, many children born of polygamous 'marriages' were legitimate in *shari'a* law, but illegitimate in state law. What the jurists principally fear, when Muslims live under non-Muslim law, is the reverse – a disastrous process that could destroy the very fabric of the Muslim family and therefore of Muslim society.

Today all but one of the colonial empires that once governed a large part of the Islamic world have ended. Even the last, the Soviet Union, appears to be drawing to a close, though currently its fifty or sixty million Muslims, most of them in old Muslim lands, are still subject to non-Muslim authority and to social and legal systems that are very remote from Muslim holy law. Even after the breakup of these empires, by no means all Muslim populations are under Muslim rule. Two non-Muslim countries, China and Ethiopia, have ruled over Muslim populations for many centuries. Among the new states established after the fall of empire, several non-Muslim countries retain significant Muslim populations, notably India, Sri Lanka, Israel, and a number of Sub-Saharan African states. Most if not all of these have been willing to maintain the system of devolution and legal autonomy, at least in matters of personal status, bequeathed to them by the empires. Their position in this is significantly different from that of the Muslim remnant in ex-Ottoman south-eastern Europe.

To these one must now add an entirely new category – Muslim minority communities formed by voluntary migration from Muslim lands to predominantly Christian countries, which have never at any time formed a part of the House of Islam. For such an action by Muslims there is no precedent in Islamic history, no previous discussion in Islamic legal literature. The jurists, ancient and modern, discussed the predicament of the Muslim under a non-Muslim government under several headings: the new convert, alienated from his previous co-religionists; the temporary visitor, taken as a captive or travelling as an envoy or a trader; the unhappy inhabitant of a Muslim country conquered by unbelievers. Not surprisingly, the possibility never seems to have entered their minds that a Muslim would voluntarily leave a Muslim land in order to place himself in this predicament. There have always been individuals and even small groups – students, political exiles, traders in this position. However until recently they were few in number and not remotely comparable with the endless flow through the centuries of travellers of every kind from Christendom to the lands of Islam. A mass migration, a reverse *hijra* of ordinary people seeking a new life among the unbelievers is an entirely new phenomenon that poses fundamental major problems. The debate on these problems has only just begun. The most common argument offered in defence of such migration is *darūra*, necessity, interpreted in economic terms. Some have tried to adduce a prophetic precedent for their action by citing the example of the Prophet who, before the *hijra*, authorized some of his Muslim followers in Mecca to seek refuge in Christian Ethiopia. That is to say that the Prophet himself had authorized the migration of Muslims to a Christian country. Others reply that they were leaving a pagan, not a Muslim city, and that no Muslim state existed at that time. The flight to Ethiopia does not therefore set a precedent for voluntary migration from a Muslim to a Christian country.

One may wonder how far the new Muslim immigrants to Christian and post-Christian lands – many of them of limited education – are aware of these juridical arguments and of the legal and theological texts on which they are based. It does not greatly matter. These texts are evidence of the concerns, beliefs and aspirations of the community from which they came. For outsider they are the most accessible, the most reliable and often the only source of information. For insiders, these texts and the simpler tracts and homilies based on them are only one of the channels through which the living tradition of the community is transmitted to them. There are many others: the home, the school, the mosque, the marketplace, and the company of their peers. One of the lessons to be learned from these texts is the capacity of the tradition, in the past, to confront new problems and to respond to them in unexpected ways.

Last year, while I was in Paris, I was invited to participate in a television programme discussing books. The following day, a

young man in a shop where I went to make a purchase recognized
me and remarked that he had seen me on television talking about
Islam. He then made an observation that has been puzzling me
ever since. 'My father', he said, 'was a Muslim, but I am a Parisian.'
What, I wondered, did he mean – that Islam is a place? Or that
Paris is a religion? As stated, obviously neither proposition is true.
Yet, as implied, neither is completely false. Their interacting implications reflect the dilemma of a minority, most of them from the
less modernized parts of their own societies of origin, who now
find themselves in a situation where they differ from the majority
among whom they live, not only because they profess a different
religion, but also because they hold a radically different concept of
what religion means, demands, and defines.

2

A FUTURE FOR THE DUTCH 'ETHNIC MINORITIES' MODEL?

HAN ENTZINGER

Integration models in Europe

Nearly all countries in Western Europe have been countries of immigration for some time now. A growing part of their populations is of recent immigrant origin. This does not imply, however, that these countries have been dealing with the social and political effects of immigration in the same way. In very broad terms, three different models may be distinguished in Europe.

Guestworker model

The first model emphasises the migrants' role in the labour market, where they tend to be seen as a conjunctural buffer. In essence, their presence is seen as temporary and no real need is felt to incorporate them into the receiving society. Of course, as time goes by and as a second generation has been growing up, a certain degree of integration has occurred. However, it may take much longer before the immigrants and their offspring are really seen as an integral part of the nation. The predominantly Germanic countries in Europe (Germany, Austria and Switzerland) are the most outspoken examples of this first model, which could be labelled as the guestworker model.

Assimilation model

In the second model immigration tends to be seen not as temporary, but as permanent. The idea here is that immigrants should be incorporated into the receiving society as quickly as possible, on the conditions set by the receiving society. A major instrument for this is the legal system, which differentiates only marginally between newcomers and the original population. Naturalization, for instance, is a quick and relatively easy procedure. This assimilation model, of which France offers the most classical example, can be particularly successful for those migrants who are willing and able to adapt to their new cultural surroundings, but it does not always work for those who tend to preserve their own cultural background.

Ethnic minorities model

It is precisely this last difficulty which is absent in the third model. The ethnic minorities model can cope more readily with cultural differences. An important element in the definition of immigrants is their different cultural identity; conditions are set that enable them to preserve this. This requires a degree of institutional pluralism, for which a political, if not a legal basis must be provided by the state. Outside the public sphere, however, equal opportunity is much harder to achieve. Sooner or later most European countries that have opted for this model (the Scandinavian and Benelux countries as well as the UK) have been faced with serious employment problems among their immigrant communities.

This chapter does not aim to compare the merits of the three models; I shall rather be dealing with the merits of one of them, the ethnic minorities model. I shall do so by reconstructing the recent history of the integration policy of the Netherlands, which together with Sweden's, has often been cited as the prototype of how immigrants can be successfully integrated without having to deny their cultural heritage. Developments that have taken place during the last two or three years, however, have been casting doubts on this presumed Dutch success story. In times of economic constraints and political uncertainties it appears more difficult to reconcile the notions of multi-culturalism with equal opportunity. The Dutch example shows that a welfare state in crisis has problems in handling immigration and integration in a multi-cultural way.

Immigrants in the Netherlands

On 1 January 1992 almost 1.3 million people living in the Netherlands, or 8.5 per cent of the population of 15.2 million, had been born abroad, and would therefore logically qualify as immigrants. Just over half of these immigrants were foreign citizens (see Table 2.1). The other half were foreign citizens who had become naturalized and Netherlands citizens originating from (former) overseas territories. They are all included in the total of 2.4 million residents of the Netherlands who either are immigrants themselves or have at least one parent born abroad and who, in that case, qualify as second generation immigrants. Thus, one in every six inhabitants of the Netherlands has direct roots in another country. This contradicts the common view that the Netherlands, just like the other countries of Western Europe, is not an immigration country. In fact, in the USA, traditionally considered the prototype immigration country of the world, the share of foreign born is now roughly of the same order as in Western Europe. (Entzinger and Carter, 1989)

The origins of the immigrant population in the Netherlands are more varied than in most other countries of Europe. This is because immigration in the last few decades has had a wide variety of causes. Some have to do with the country's colonial past, others with the needs of its labour market, and some migrants have been admitted for humanitarian reasons. (Entzinger, 1985; Penninx *et*

Table 2.1. Non-Dutch residents in the Netherlands, by selected categories, 1976-1993 (1 January selected years)

	EC*	Turkey	Morocco	Total
1976	112,700	76,500	42,200	350,500
1981	134,000	138,500	83,400	520,900
1986	135,000	156,400	116,400	552,500
1991	168,400	203,500	156,900	692,400
1992	176,200	214,800	163,700	732,900
1993	183,600	213,000	165,500	756,500

*Belgium, Denmark, France, Germany (FR), Greece (only from 1986), Ireland, Italy, Luxembourg, Portugal (from 1991), Spain (from 1991), United Kingdom

Source: Central Bureau for Statistics, The Netherlands.

al., 1993) After a relative low in the first half of the 20th century, immigration gained momentum in the aftermath of World War II. The independence of Indonesia in 1949, until then the most important Dutch colony, led to the departure of between 250,000 and 300,000 Netherlands citizens, colonizers of European descent as well as people of mixed origin. Most of them settled in the 'mother country', which many had never visited before. In that same period about 400,000 Netherlands citizens left their country to settle in classical immigration countries like Canada and Australia. It was not until 1961 that the migration balance of the Netherlands became positive for the first time, later than in most other Western European states. Since that year the migration surplus has remained, with the year 1967 as the only exception.

Like elsewhere in the north-west of Europe, the 1960s and early 1970s were the years of recruitment of unskilled workers in a number of countries around the Mediterranean. Here, the Netherlands made a rather late start, and this is why relatively few 'guest workers' came from Southern Europe and relatively many from more distant countries, in particular from Turkey and Morocco. The share of foreign workers in the Dutch labour force has never been as high as in neighbouring countries. This is because the country has little heavy industry and no coal mining. Moreover, the relatively high birth rates of those days kept the domestic labour force at a satisfactory level. As in other European countries, and contrary to the original idea, many foreign workers did not return home. They have remained in the Netherlands and in many cases they have been joined by their families.

The recruitment of labour outside the European Union has been insignificant for the past two decades, but immigration from previous recruitment countries still continues. At present many members of the so-called second generation find their marriage partners in the country from which their parents originate. This phenomenon is particularly evident among the Turks and the Moroccans who, with 240,000 and 195,000 members respectively (citizens plus naturalized citizens), constitute the two largest immigrant communities. In 1992 alone about 18,000 Turks and Moroccans arrived to live in the Netherlands. Return migration to these two countries is almost negligible, but as acquiring Netherlands citizenship has become more popular in recent years, the number of Turkish and Moroccan citizens residing in the Netherlands is now growing much more slowly than the number of those whose ethnic origins lie in these countries.

A third major immigration movement of the last decades stems from the Caribbean. Surinam, which was a part of the kingdom until its independence in 1975, saw more than one third of its potential population leave for the Netherlands. At present the number of people of Surinamese descent in the Netherlands is estimated at 260,000. Nearly all of them hold Netherlands citizenship. There are also about 90,000 people from the Netherlands Antilles (Curaçao and some smaller islands) and Aruba living in the Netherlands. These two small states are autonomous parts of the kingdom, their inhabitants all possess Netherlands citizenship and are free to settle in the Netherlands.

The multicultural approach of 'temporary' migration

There are important differences in the way public policymakers have dealt with the various categories of immigrants. However, one major characteristic of official policy, was that until 1980 the idea prevailed that the Netherlands was not a country of immigration. The major argument to support this approach was the country's already dense population. Besides, many migrants themselves were convinced that one day they would return home. Rotation, in fact, was the idea behind the 'guest worker' policy, as it had been adopted by the Netherlands and other Western European countries. Also for those who had come from (former) colonies – with the exception of most migrants from Indonesia – the notion of return migration persisted, often upon completion of their education in the 'mother country'. In reality, many migrants continued to postpone their return or did not return at all. It took a while before the Dutch, including their government, had understood that in migration the return myth might have an important ideological function for migrant communities, but that it might always remain a myth.

Although the authorities did not consider the Netherlands to be a country of immigration, a policy was designed that aimed at promoting the 'well being' of the 'temporary guests'. As in many other countries, the 1960s and 1970s were years of rapid expansion of the welfare state and the social security system and years of professionalization of social work and social services. Migrants were first of all seen as people in need of care. Therefore, social work agencies, fully subsidized by the state, began to play an important role in the reception and counselling of immigrants. In line with the idea of temporariness, they were approached in accordance with rules and habits of their own culture. It was expected that this would facilitate their reinsertion upon return. With this same idea in mind, mother-tongue teaching was introduced in primary education in 1974, when family reunification had begun to gain momentum. These efforts to preserve the migrants' cultural heritage reflect the tradition of the Netherlands as a multicultural society with its institutionalized social and religious diversity, commonly known as 'pillarization'. (Lijphart, 1975)

As the 1970s drew to an end, it became increasingly clear that a substantial number of immigrants would not return. A political debate on forced return migration was quickly abandoned with the argument that migrant workers had contributed so significantly to the development of Dutch economy that it would be immoral to send them home against their will. Those who had come from former colonies could not be forced to return either, not only because of their Netherlands citizenship, but also because of certain feelings of guilt, which were rather generally felt by many Dutch people over the colonial past.

In this same period there was a clear increase in the number of immigrants, primarily as a result of family reunification, and they became more and more visible in daily life. More or less simultaneously, their labour market situation deteriorated. As a result of economic restructuring and selective dismissals, unemployment among immigrants went up more steeply than among the native population. Moreover, some terrorist acts, including two train hijackings, carried out by young Moluccans – a relatively small group from the former Netherlands East Indies – forced the authorities to take immigration and its social consequences more seriously.

In 1979 the Scientific Council for Government Policy (WRR), an independent advisory body to the Prime Minister of the Netherlands, published a report that recommended abandoning the fiction of temporary residence and developing integration policy for the immigrants. (WRR, 1979) The aim of such a policy would be to promote the migrants' fuller participation in social and economic life, as well as to develop good inter-ethnic relations. At the same time, migrants should be given a chance to develop their cultural identity insofar as this would not hamper their integration.

Minorities policy of the 1980s

The report of the Scientific Council marked an important change in the thinking about immigration, not only in public opinion, but also in official policy. In 1980 the government formally admitted that the idea that most immigrants would eventually return should be abandoned. A stricter admissions policy was also announced. Moreover, the government decided to set up a coordinated policy for the 'ethnic minorities'. It was around this time that this concept began to penetrate into public speech, although the new 'Minorities Policy' was not formally launched until 1983. The Minister of the Interior was given special coordinating competence for this policy, even though all ministers remained responsible for its application in their own respective fields (*Minderhedennota*, 1983). It should be made clear that, in official use, the concept of 'ethnic minority' is a synonym neither for 'immigrants' nor for 'foreigners'. The peculiarity of this concept is that it combines the cultural notion of a non-Dutch ethnic origin with the idea of a minority position. Minority position should be understood both in its quantitative meaning (a small group) and in its sociological meaning: a relatively deprived group in the margins of society. Finally, the term reflects a sense of community and togetherness, assumed to be a characteristic of the different groups of immigrant origin.

Minorities Policy does not apply to all immigrant communities, but only to those 'for whose presence the government feels a special responsibility (because of the colonial past or because they had been recruited by the authorities), and who find themselves in a minority situation' (*Minderhedennota*, 1983: 12). This includes the following groups: Surinamese, Antilleans and Arubans, Moluccans, Turks, Moroccans, Italians, Spaniards, Portuguese, Greeks, (former) Yugoslavs, Tunisians, Cape Verdians, gypsies, recognized political refugees and tinkers (an indigenous semi-nomadic group that had already been subject to a special government policy for a long time). When Minorities Policy was designed in 1980, these groups together totalled 450,000 people. Since then their numbers have more than doubled (see Table 2.2). The careful observer will note that the Dutch of Indonesian origin are not seen as an ethnic minority; there is a general impression that they have quickly become assimilated. Also, communities originating from nearby countries have never been given minority status. They are not in a situation of social deprivation.

Table 2.2 Ethnic minorities in the Netherlands, 1 January 1992
(as defined by the Ministry of the Interior)

Turks	240.200 (1)
Moroccans	194.800 (1)
Italians	32.200 (1)
Spaniards	28.600 (1)
Yugoslavs	26.600 (1)
Portuguese	20.100 (1)
Cape Verdians	14.600 (1)
Greeks	9.900 (1)
Tunisian	2.500 (2)
Surinamese	263.700 (1)
Antillians/Arubans	91.500 (1)
Refugees	40.200 (3)
Moluccans	40.000 (4)
Tinkers	30.000 (4)
Gypsies	3.500 (4)
Total	1.038.400

Notes:

(1) On the basis of ethnic origin (i.e. born outside the Netherlands
    and/or one or both parents born outside the Netherlands).
(2) On the basis of citizenship.
(3) Persons with official refugee status, as estimated by NIDI.
(4) Data provided by the Ministry of Social Welfare (WVC).

Source: Nederlands Centrum Buitenlanders, 1993: 21.

The three major elements of Minorities Policy are:

1. promoting multi-culturalism and emancipation of ethnic
   communities;
2. promoting equality before the law;
3. overcoming social and economic deprivation by promoting
   equal opportunity.

Thus, the situation of the ethnic minorities was defined simultaneously in social, economic, cultural and legal terms. Attempts to
improve their situation should take all these aspects into account.
Traditionally, however, a relatively heavy weight was given to the
first aspect, the promotion of multi-culturalism.

Promoting multi-culturalism

The notion of multi-culturalism finds its origins in a society that sees itself made up of groups and communities rather than of individuals. It can be understood as a continuation of the Dutch tradition of religious, social and cultural pluralism, as it had become institutionalized under the 'pillarization' system in the days before immigration was gaining significance. Under this heading, the policy of the 1970s, which aimed at preserving and developing migrant cultures, was continued. Mother tongue teaching, for instance, was given a legal basis and it was intensified in both private and public schools. More recently, however, as doubts have been growing about its effectiveness, it has again been slightly reduced. (Lucassen and Köbben, 1992)

Dutch law also allows for the establishment of private schools of any religious denomination, entirely subsidized by public money. In the past five years about twenty Muslim schools have been set up in various parts of the country on the basis of this law, as well as some Hindu schools. Their status is equal to that of Roman Catholic, Protestant and Jewish schools. In those schools, all of which are at primary level, teaching takes place in Dutch and the curriculum is in accordance with the directives prescribed by the authorities. It should be noted that only a small minority of Muslim and Hindu immigrants (the latter coming mainly from Surinam) send their children to these schools.

Another relevant measure in this context is the establishment of consultative councils for each of the major ethnic minorities. Such councils have been created at national level by the Ministry of the Interior, as well as at the local level, particularly in cities with substantial immigrant concentrations. Like almost everywhere else in Europe, the largest immigrant concentrations are to be found in the metropolitan areas. Forty-five per cent of all ethnic minorities live in the four major cities of the Netherlands (Amsterdam, Rotterdam, The Hague and Utrecht), as against a mere thirteen per cent of the population as a whole. (see Table 2.3) The members of these consultative councils are delegates of the major immigrant associations. The authorities are obliged to consult them on any measure that affects the minorities.

In more general terms, the authorities attempt to promote the creation of ethnic associations and organizations at local, regional and national levels. Such associations may pursue a variety of aims, ranging from sports activities, social counselling, language courses

Table 2.3. Ethnic breakdown of the population of the four major cities of
the Netherlands, 1st January 1991

	Amsterdam	Rotterdam	The Hague	Utrecht
All inhabitants (A)	702,731	582,242	444,181	231,570
Turkish citizens	24,128	28,449	16,798	7,840
Moroccan citizens	33,902	17,202	12,950	13,101
All non-Dutch cit.(B)	108,861	72,579	53,609	27,869
Origins in Surinam/				
Neth.Ant./Aruba (C)	61,679	45,533	34,564	6,876
B as % of A	15.5	12.5	12.1	13.4
(B+C) as % of A	24.3	20.3	19.9	15.0

Source: Muus, 1991: 29.

(both Dutch and mother tongue), to producing radio and television programmes. Subsidizing religious activities is legally forbidden. Certain publicly subsidized activities, however, such as
language courses, may take place in mosques.

Equality before the law

The second element of Minorities Policy aims at achieving equality
before the law. This is achieved by granting all foreign citizens with
a certain residence record the rights and obligations that also apply
to Netherlands citizens, with only a few exceptions. This policy
element applies to all foreign citizens, not only to those who are
members of a recognized minority group. In addition to this, the
combat against racism and discrimination has been identified. To
this purpose, the Penal Code has been amended and reinforced. In
the Netherlands there is no specific legislation that aims at promoting better inter-ethnic relations, as in Britain, the USA and some
other countries. The impression is that existing anti-discrimination
legislation is adequate, although not always easy to apply in
concrete cases.

In the 1980s the rights of non-Dutch citizens were gradually
extended. First, several pieces of legislation that relate to cultural
and religious practices were altered to accommodate certain non-
Christian or non-Jewish rites (e.g. in funerals or in slaughtering).
Foreign residents are now also allowed to enter the Dutch public
service (with some minor exceptions like the police and the
armed forces).

Table 2.4 Foreigners taking up Netherlands citizenship, by selected previous nationalities, 1992.

	Numbers	Per 1,000 of resident population
Turkey	11.495	54
Morocco	7.976	49
Surinam*	5.115	236
(ex-) Yugoslavia	1.074	71
Cape Verde	331	120
Tunisia	272	106
Portugal	107	12
Italy	92	5
Greece	79	15
Spain	62	4
All nationalities	36.170	49

*For Surinamese who were Netherlands citizens until 1975 a simplified and shortened naturalisation procedure is applicable.

Source: Ministry of Justice/Central Bureau of Statistics, The Netherlands

The most interesting example here is the granting of active and passive voting rights to foreign citizens with a residence record of at least five years. However, the right to vote and to be elected is limited to the municipal, and, in some of the larger cities, to the district levels. Participation in provincial and national elections remains reserved for Netherlands citizens. In the local elections of 1986 and 1990 a few dozen foreigners were elected to municipal councils, particularly in the larger cities and in border regions. In both years the participation rate among foreigners remained below the overall average. The large majority of those who did vote voted for one of the established Dutch parties and not for immigrant parties.

It is interesting to note that in spite of this policy of promoting equal treatment of Dutch and foreign citizens, the number of naturalizations has gone up substantially during the past few years. In 1992 more than 36,000 foreign citizens obtained Netherlands citizenship, which corresponds to almost 5 per cent of the foreign population of the country. Many foreign citizens have a rather instrumental reason for their application: a Netherlands passport generally guarantees uncomplicated travelling in Europe and other parts of the world. The naturalization procedure is relatively uncomplicated and not very expensive (Ecu 170 as a maximum). The main requirement is five years of uninterrupted stay in the Netherlands; less strict requirements apply to spouses and partners of Netherlands citizens. Recently the government has decided to allow dual citizenship, which means that foreigners who have become naturalized no longer have to abandon their old citizenship (Van den Bedem, 1993).

Equal opportunity

This third element of Minorities Policy to combat social and economic deprivation has been considerably less successful than the two others. The aim here is to promote the minorities' participation in the major fields and institutions of society up to a level that corresponds to their share in the total population, whether at local, regional or national level. This idea of proportional 'representation' reflects the typically Dutch idea that ethnic origin, culture or religion should not affect the possibility of participating in economic and social life: there should be equal opportunity for all.

In reality developments have been a lot more varied, and also rather differentiated by sector and by minority group. In the field of housing, for instance, the situation of most immigrants has substantially improved over the past ten years. The quality of minority housing is now practically the same as for the Dutch population of a similar social and economic background. This improvement has been enhanced by the essentially non-discriminatory distribution system for social housing, which in the largest cities includes the vast majority of all housing (Van Dugteren, 1993).

In education and employment the situation is much less positive. Although school achievements for the second generation are considerably better than for the first – in particular for the Surinamese, the Antilleans and the Moluccans – the gap between minority and other children still remains wide. Frequent school drop-out, an insufficient knowledge of Dutch and discriminatory practices by employers constitute major obstacles for the successful entrance of these youngsters into the labour market. It is precisely in the labour market that the situation is worst. The unemployment rate among Turks and Moroccans stands, depending on the definition chosen, at between 21 and 36 per cent of the labour force. For the Surinamese and the Antilleans the corresponding figure lies between 17 and 31 per cent, whereas only 7 per cent of the non-immigrant population is unemployed. (Sociaal en Cultureel Planbureau, 1992: 66; Tesser, 1993) In the past few years the latter number has gradually gone down, while minority percentages have remained high, in spite of numerous efforts to promote their integration in the labour market.

Obviously this difference between minorities and majority is partly explained by differences in the average level of training and education. This difference in starting positions is sometimes overlooked by the authorities when they compare the social situation of the various ethnic minorities (Delcroix, 1991). Nevertheless, also when the statistics are corrected for such differences, the labour force participation of ethnic minorities remains well below that of the Dutch with a corresponding educational level. More than ten years of Minorities Policy have not led to any improvement in this crucial area, even though this can partly be seen as an effect of continuing immigration, which accounts for a steady inflow of people who are insufficiently qualified for the Dutch labour market. Specific instruments, such as improved vocational training, intensified employment services, special job programmes and others have not been very successful. Moreover, in the past ten years the number of unskilled jobs has diminished as a result of a fundamental restructuring of the Dutch economy. Most minority groups are faced with a wide gap between supply and demand in the labour market, and their employment prospects are not very hopeful.

The turn of the early 1990s: more emphasis on integration

For a long time the negative social effects of persistent high unemployment among ethnic minorities have been insufficiently acknowledged. The minorities' full entitlement to social security benefits was considered an acceptable alternative that enabled those affected by unemployment to live a decent life. As in the 1970s, many Dutchmen still see minorities as objects of welfare state care, rather than as a labour market potential. Only in recent years has an awareness been growing that such an approach is not only paternalistic, but that it also encourages a process of marginalization among certain minority communities. A considerable number of immigrants, for instance, still do not speak Dutch, even after twenty or more years of residence. Many have hardly ever met a Dutch person and withdraw into their own communities. Many are not in a position to structure their lives because they lack the daily rhythm that a regular job imposes upon the individual. Under such circumstances the challenge offered by fundamentalism or by crime may serve as a substitute in cases where there are no other opportunities that would enable ethnic minority members to familiarize themselves with the society that surrounds them.

At the same time, this surrounding society is not always aware of the cultural bias that is inherent in any system through which goods and services are distributed. The school system, the labour market, social and cultural services all tend to disadvantage those members of a society who are less familiar with the rules and regulations that govern such institutions and their functioning. This phenomenon is generally known as discrimination. A distinction can be made between conscious or deliberate discrimination on the one hand, where differential treatment and disadvantaging of certain groups or individuals is an explicit aim, and non-deliberate discrimination on the other hand. Here, differential treatment is not an aim, but an effect of the application of existing rules. There is a growing awareness in Dutch society, as well as among the authorities, that the cumulative effects of non-deliberate discrimination against ethnic minorities can be quite strong, and that this accounts to a large extent for the persistent unemployment. Therefore, it is now felt that the search for policy measures to counter these effects must be intensified.

This rather gloomy analysis of the situation of ethnic minorities is largely based on the second report on this subject that was presented by the Scientific Council for Government Policy to the government in 1989, ten years after the Council's first report (WRR, 1989). In this second report the Scientific Council argued that not only would the immigrants' presence be permanent, but also that immigration itself had become a permanent feature in West European societies. Immigration, according to the Council, would continue as long as the gap between the poor and the rich persisted at world level. Besides, immigration is enhanced by the presence of substantial immigrant communities in Europe. In the Council's view, introducing more restrictions in immigration policy would only have a marginal effect.

As regards future Minorities Policy, the Scientific Council recommended that more emphasis should be placed on economic and social integration, in particular in the labour market, education and vocational training. In the view of the Council, a country that admits immigrants should also offer them an opportunity to develop further their capacities, so that they can be self-supporting, rather than having to rely on the social security system for the remainder of their potential working lives. To achieve this aim, the Council proposed a number of policy instruments, such as, for instance, a major intensification of language training, in some cases even compulsory, a 'welcome policy' for newly arrived immigrants, as well as an improvement of teaching methods of Dutch as a second language in primary education.

The Council also recommended the introduction of certain forms of positive action in the labour market, including a legal obligation for employers to report publicly on their efforts to recruit members of ethnic minority groups. Such a law would be similar to the Employment Equity Law that Canada has known since the mid-1980s. This law does not prescribe any quotas; it is meant to encourage employers to be more conscious about the possible negative effects on ethnic minorities of their traditional recruitment practices and personnel policies. The Council suggests that changing some of their procedures and making some additional effort would give them better access to the immigrant potential in the labour market. If this potential is neglected, the general employment situation will worsen, particularly in the larger cities with their high numbers of young people of immigrant origin. Positive action should be distinguished from positive discrimination: under positive action entry requirements should never be lowered, as this would quickly backfire all members of the group concerned.

It is very obvious that in the four years since the publication of the Scientific Council's second report the appreciation of immigration as well as the political discourse in this area has changed (Nederlands Gesprek Centrum, 1992). Some of the measures proposed by the Council have already been implemented, although mostly in an experimental form. New measures include the introduction of language classes on a much larger scale than before, as well as the setting up of monitoring systems for newly arrived immigrants in a number of cities. On 1 July 1993, the Second (i.e. Lower) Chamber of Parliament passed the Law on Employment Equity, roughly along the lines proposed by the Scientific Council.

A review of the three elements of Minorities Policy over the past ten years indicates a gradual shift towards the third element, the promotion of social and economic integration through a policy of equal opportunity. Unfortunately, this policy can hardly be called successful up to now. Successes have been much more spectacular in the legal field. By now all major measures meant to promote equality before the law have been put into practice. At first the promoting of multi-culturalism led to some remarkable successes, but this policy element has lost some of its significance over the past ten years. In fact subsidies for social and cultural activities of ethnic minorities have been reduced or discontinued, mother tongue teaching has become more disputed, and establishing ethnic and immigrant organizations as well as encouraging other initiatives from among these communities are now largely seen as the responsibility of the immigrants themselves rather than the authorities.

Since the autumn of 1991 the public debate on immigration and the future of ethnic minorities has been intensified. These issues are much higher on the political agenda than before. The change was provoked by Mr Frits Bolkestein, parliamentary leader of the VVD, the conservative liberal party (Bolkestein, 1991). Some of his observations on the subject were without the usual reserve typical until then of public debate in this field so full of taboos. Public attitudes towards immigration and multi-culturalism appear to have become harsher – some would say more realistic – among certain parts of the population. The tone of a public discussion on illegal immigrants that took place in the aftermath of the Amsterdam air crash in October 1992, reflected a degree of xenophobia that had hitherto been almost unknown in the Netherlands (Nederlands Centrum Buitenlanders, 1993). In the summer of 1993, as the numbers of asylum seekers suddenly went up, a mild form of moral panic broke out over immigration. This time the debate focused on whether the Netherlands – with its already high population density – should be considered 'full' and, on that basis, should opt for a stricter immigration policy.

Up to now no strong right-wing anti-immigrant movement has developed in the Netherlands, comparable to the Front National in France, the Vlaams Blok in Belgium or the Republikaner in Germany. The anti-immigrant 'Centrumpartij' has only one seat out of 150 in the Second Chamber of Parliament as well as a few seats in the city councils of the largest towns. Considerable gains, however, are generally expected in the parliamentary elections scheduled for May 1994. In the past few years the number of attacks on asylum centres and islamic institutions has also increased, but unlike most surrounding countries the Netherlands has so far been saved from violent clashes between groups of immigrants and the original population or between immigrants and the police.

Conclusion: a future for the 'ethnic minorities' model?

It is evident that in the Netherlands the immigration issue and, above all, the future of multi-culturalism is currently being reassessed. It is believed that a strategy of achieving equality before the law and respect for immigrant cultures has not prevented processes of social marginalization from taking place. So far, the provisions of the welfare state, traditionally well developed in the Netherlands, may by and large have avoided ghettoization and serious poverty among immigrants. At the same time, however, these provisions have enhanced the immigrants' dependency on public support and discouraged many of them to familiarize themselves with the demands of modern Dutch society.

Although certain members of the second generation have successfully settled on an integration course, large segments of the Turkish and Moroccan communities in the Netherlands are clearly in a minority situation, characterized by a low degree of social and cultural integration and a high dependency on welfare state provisions. To a much lesser extent this is the case for immigrants of Surinamese and Antillean origin. Quite clearly, integration takes time. Some recent trends and developments, however, make it doubtful whether enough time will be available. These trends all seem to be inspired by a growing interdependence at the European, if not at the global level, and it would be difficult for public authorities to ignore them.

The first of these trends is the perceived rise in immigration. Although immigration to the Netherlands has seen its ups and downs throughout the last few decades, one may say that it has reached a structurally higher level in recent years. To some extent this is an effect of the sizeable immigrant communities present in the Netherlands and in Western Europe as a whole, which act as bridgeheads for further immigration. The rise in immigration also stems from changes on the international political scene. Since the classical East-West opposition in the world has lost its significance, it appears to be less easy to contain regional conflicts. Such conflicts, which may take place all over the world, tend to produce considerable numbers of asylum seekers and refugees, many of whom are potential immigrants. Within Europe the disappearance of the Iron Curtain has also led to some East-West labour migration, although Germany and Austria have been affected much more than the Netherlands. Other countries in Western Europe, however, including France and Britain, have seen no increase in their immigration figures. Yet, whether right or wrong, a general feeling has been spreading in Western Europe that immigration has become more difficult to control. Under such circumstances any policy that aims to integrate both newcomers and the more established immigrant communities is liable to meet with opposition, this is even more so for policies that claim respect for immigrant cultures.

The second recent trend is a major change in the structures of most West European economies, including that of the Netherlands. High labour costs and technological innovation appear to be forcing most Western European economies into another round of 'rationalization' and automation, as in the early 1980s, thus making more unskilled labour redundant. There is also increased competition from low-wage economies in other parts of the world. This process has a relatively strong impact on people of immigrant origin, given their generally low skill levels. It is particularly painful for new immigrants, many of whom cannot be accommodated in these shrinking segments of the labour market. The paradox is, however, that some other segments of the labour market tend to employ new immigrants illegally at wage levels and labour conditions that are far below the statutory requirements. Illegal employment, however, has a negative impact on employment opportunities in the formal economy, especially at the lower skill levels, and it strongly undermines ideas of equal opportunity for all.

A third trend, not unrelated to previous one, is the mounting pressure on the provisions of the welfare state. In the political debate in a number of European countries, including the Netherlands, a consensus seems to be emerging that the price of social security is becoming too high. An important reason for this is the worsening worker/non-worker ratio. The number of contributors to the system tends to go down, whereas the number of beneficiaries has been going up. This trend is induced by the ageing of the labour force, by a growing incidence of early retirement and by high labour costs. A rise in un(der)employment nearly always affects immigrants more strongly than the average population. Therefore, their reliance on the social security system also tends to move up to higher than average. Basically, growing pressure on the social security system and on other provisions of the welfare state can be relieved in two ways. One is an overall lowering of the benefits, which would lead to further marginalization of immigrant communities. The other is a more selective approach, which, for example, would grant fewer rights to new entrants into the social security system. Among these new entrants, immigrants and people of immigrant origin tend to be overrepresented. Both solutions clearly run counter to the notion of equal opportunity, irrespective of ethnic or cultural origins (Entzinger, 1994).

These three trends appear to be converging and even tend to reinforce one another. Recent developments in the Netherlands seem to indicate that claiming respect for immigrants and their cultures is now becoming increasingly difficult. A relatively successful combination of achieving equality according to the law and promoting multi-culturalism has not prevented a process of social marginalization among large segments of the immigrant population. It looks as though multi-culturalism has better chances as long as immigration is perceived as manageable and as long as the contribution of immigrant communities to a country's economy is clear. Neither the legal nor the multi-cultural approach have proved to be a sufficient guarantee for successful social and economic integration.

The Dutch case illustrates some of the difficulties of the ethnic minorities model. The material presented here does not allow for any conclusions on the merits of the other two models presented at the beginning of this chapter, the guest worker and the assimilation model. Given the current situation of many immigrants and people of immigrant origin elsewhere in Europe, one might be tempted to think that none of the three models offer a perfect solution. Does this mean that there is no way at all of integrating immigrants into an established society? That conclusion would be one bridge too far: many societies in the world have given sufficient evidence of the opposite.

In many cases both in the past and in the present, integration of immigrants has proved to be possible, but so far there has been only a limited experience with integration processes in welfare states with a strong public sector, as in most of present-day Western Europe. In a welfare state public authorities dispose of relatively strong steering mechanisms, meant to promote and maintain social integration not only by guaranteeing a social minimum for all, but in many cases also by striving for equal opportunity, irrespective of class, ethnic, regional origins or other characteristics based on ascription rather than achievement. Equal opportunity is already difficult to bring about in non-immigrant situations where a relatively broad consensus on basic values exists. In those cases where such a consensus is absent, and where a democratic state does not consider it its task to enforce a particular culture plus the subsequent behaviour upon its subjects, it becomes next to impossible. Stripped to their essential characteristics, promoting multi-culturalism in a modern welfare state seems to be irreconcilable with the notion of equal opportunity for all. Pursuing only one of these two aims and completely neglecting the other, however, may easily be taken as discriminatory and, therefore, will not lead to social integration either. This is the basic dilemma of multi-culturalism and the welfare state, and therefore of the Dutch 'ethnic minorities' approach to immigration. For the time being, finding the perfect mix very much seems a matter of trial and error, as the Netherlands has begun to discover in the recent past.

3

ISLAM AND MUSLIM CIVIL RIGHTS IN THE NETHERLANDS

JOHANNES J.G. JANSEN

In the wake of the death sentence that Khomeini pronounced on Salman Rushdie, on 3 and 4 March 1989 Muslims in the Netherlands held public demonstrations in two large Dutch cities, The Hague and Rotterdam. The demonstrators supported the death sentence. This came as a shock to the Dutch public and elaborate discussions followed, both in parliament, on 7 March, and in the press. Many of the contributions were phrased in firm language of the 'and here we should draw the line' type. Other contributors to the discussion, on the contrary, even alleged to have unmasked the Dutch government and proclaimed to have demonstrated that the Dutch government 'rejected Islam categorically' (Haleber, 1989). In a secular society this was a serious charge indeed.

However, since the anti-Rushdie demonstrations of March 1989 and the public discussion which followed, the Dutch public now realizes that Islam is a religion that is not only professed in remote corners of the Third World; Islam is also professed in the Netherlands.

With most people, religions other than their own usually evoke suspicion. The Dutch are no exception. When a religion grows stronger, the suspicion becomes stronger as well. The demonstrations in March were understood as a show of strength. Against all publicly accepted views on freedom of expression that exist in that country, the Muslims in the Netherlands had dared to claim the right to forbid a book which they regarded as anti-Islamic. Could such deviation from the Dutch norms be allowed? Did these people think they were strong enough to forbid a Dutch citizen to read what he wanted to read? Did this minority know its place? What exactly should this place be? Where did these Muslims come from?

The five Muslim communities that exist in the Netherlands did not come there for religious reasons. They did not emigrate from their countries of origin because of a desire to live a perfect Islamic life; they departed for a variety of mundane reasons. Nevertheless, they nowadays regard many of the difficulties that they encounter as related to their religion, and somehow connected to Islam.

Both the members of these communities and members of the (non-Muslim) Dutch public now show symptoms of what the American scholar Ralph Linton (1942) once called 'nativism': they think of their own culture as being endangered by others, and look for distinctive elements within their own culture that should be emphasized, or revived, in order to be able to feel fortified against these others. To Muslims this process is relatively easy: what, within their own culture, is more distinctive than Islam and its precepts? To the non-Muslims, on the other hand, it is not easy to identify the culturally distinctive elements of their own world: obviously Christianity to which they bade farewell a generation ago, will not do, but how about tolerance, separation of religion and politics, Calvinist work ethic, the recently discoverd equality of men and women, or, perhaps, even monogamy? The Dutch press daily provides testimony of the fierce struggle taking place in the hearts and minds of Dutch opinion leaders, and it is the Muslim presence in the Netherlands that has provoked this soul-searching.

The Moluccans are the oldest Muslim group in the Netherlands. They arrived in the late 1940s and the early 1950s. They were being repatriated from the Royal Dutch Indian Army when the Republic of Indonesia gradually overthrew Dutch rule over its territory in its war of independence. At the time most Moluccans expected to return to their homelands quickly.

To this day many of them have not given up this dream. In the early 1960s two other groups started to arrive from Turkey and Morocco. They had been asked to come to the Netherlands to work in the rapidly expanding economy, which needed labour that could not be found locally. It was originally assumed that these three groups, the Moluccans, the Turks and the Moroccans, would eventually go back to their countries of origin once this became possible.

The Javanese and Hindustani Muslims arrived in the middle of the 1970s from Surinam, a former Dutch colony in South America, when it became independent. Many of the inhabitants of Surinam had little faith in the new post-colonial rulers and preferred to live in the Netherlands. At present about half of all Surinamese live in the Netherlands. It was never seriously expected that these Surinamese would ever return to Surinam. In the wake of the realization that the Surinamese were there to stay, the Dutch slowly started to realize that the three Muslim communities that had been established in the Netherlands before the 1980s were also a permanent phenomenon.

Modern Dutch society has effectively marginalized religion. This becomes clear when one examines where churches are built in the new towns founded on land which has been reclaimed from the sea. Whereas Dutch towns and villages are usually centered around a church, or churches, the new settlements are not. Moreover town planners refused to allow church towers to rise above the skyline of a new settlement: the honour of dominating the skyline, so they contended, should go to profane and civic buildings.

At present religion may be marginal in Dutch society, but it is firmly entrenched in the Dutch social and legal system. Religious organizations enjoy a wide range of privileges that are enshrined in law and custom. As a matter of course, Muslims have started to claim the rights that these laws and customs grant to religious communities.

To Muslims religion is not marginal; it is one of the central facts of life. To their Dutch neighbours, this is confusing. The Dutch prefer to think of the Muslim communities in the Netherlands as ethnic communities. Both the general public and the authorities define these communities according to a variety of social variables, not according to religious criteria.

This not only causes confusion, but also creates conflict. The Muslims and their organizations in the Netherlands rarely feel that they get what is due to them. They mistrust the superstructure of secular welfare work, which the Dutch authorities have created to see to their needs and solve their problems. The authorities perceive these needs as social. Education, health, unemployment and housing are the main problems to which they turn their attention.

Conversely, the Muslim population of the Netherlands defines many of its problems as religious. In this area the Dutch have a finely balanced system of liberty and constraint which has existed since the nineteenth century and which came about in the course of the struggle between the Protestants and Catholics for emancipation and social supremacy.[1]

The Muslims in the Netherlands have been gradually trying to take their place as one of the Dutch religious communities. But the Dutch authorities who had encouraged the immigration of Muslims to the Netherlands, especially during the 1960s, never expected this to happen. Only recently have they started to recognize that the situation has its own internal logic, and that it is not possible to deny one religious group the rights that are routinely given to another.

However, many obstacles have to be surmounted before the situation can be judged as satisfactory to all concerned. There is, for instance, a long list of points of conflict between Dutch law and the ideals of Muslim law. However, Muslim law is religious by nature, and since the Dutch constitution guarantees freedom of religion to everyone who resides in the Netherlands, the Dutch system can only in exceptional cases refuse to comply with demands that are justified by religious arguments.

The most obvious point in case is polygamy. Should polygamous marriages be recognized by Dutch law? Should the sacrosanct principle of the right to family reunification be applied to polygamous Muslim families? Some have argued that this should be the case. The right of families to live together is violated by the present Dutch principle of giving a legal right of residence to only one spouse (Shadid and Van Koningsveld, 1989, 1990). Muslim and Moroccan law are here in conflict with Dutch law, which recognizes an Islamic polygamous marriage but does not concede right of residence to all wives or to all children.

The application of the Dutch rules of custody of young children after a divorce is always felt by one of the parents to be one of the great injustices of this world. This is the case for ethnic Dutch couples who are divorcing, and it is even more true for Muslim couples, since Muslim law on parental custody after divorce is completely different. Dutch courts have been confronted with intricate situations where Muslims have asked them to apply Muslim family law in the matter of parental custody (Rutten, 1988).

Even in the Islamic world, the principles of Muslim law are not always applied in total. However, Muslim family law usually prevails, in one form or another. Hence, it is only natural that Muslims expect the application of Muslim family law, even from a non-Muslim government. A Dutch lawyer, Mrs S.W.E. Rutten, has published a voluminous inventory of Dutch court decisions involving Muslims and Muslim law (Rutten, 1988).

One set of rules Muslim law prescribes concerns the proper way to slaughter animals for human consumption. In their daily life, Muslims attach great value to this set of rules. When man takes the life of an animal, so Islam prescribes, he must invoke the name of God. The butcher must pronounce the formula, 'In the name of God, the Compassionate, the Merciful', *Bismillah ar-Rahman ar-Rahim*. The animal has to be killed by the cutting of its carotid arteries, which causes loss of consciousness within seconds; death follows through loss of blood.

A report published in 1984 by the Dutch Society for the Protection of Animals concludes that an animal killed in this way 'does not really suffer'. However this same report asks the Dutch authorities to forbid the Islamic method of animal slaughter, although this practice had been permitted since 1977 (Nederlandse Dierenbeschermings, 1984).

In the late 1970s and early 1980s xenophobic political groups have attempted to incite hatred of foreigners by exploiting love of animals. According to such groups, the modern industrial way of killing animals wholesale in factories is far preferable to the traditional Islamic method. At the moment, this theme is not central in discussions on Islam in the Netherlands.

Problems concerning religion in the limited European meaning of that word have equally been the subject of political debates and judicial decisions. Should the Dutch government give financial support to the establishment of mosques, in the same way that it has financed the construction of churches?[2] In 1976[3] and 1981[4] the Dutch government promulgated two 'Regulations', which gave some financial support to the building of new mosques. The two most prominent arguments used to justify these Regulations were that a mosque is not only a place of prayer but also serves important social functions within the community, and that the Muslims in the Netherlands had the right to receive that which the Church had already received. These two Regulations have financially contributed to the construction of exactly one hundred mosques (Hirsch Ballin, 1988).

When the 1981 Regulation lost its validity in 1984, the Dutch parliament[5] decided that the central government should no longer grant subsidies for the construction of mosques. Nevertheless, since then municipalities have granted such subsidies from their own budgets. Also, the central government has paid subsidies for Muslim socio-cultural activities. Such activities might, of course, include the construction of a mosque.[6]

In August 1986 a conflict arose about a mosque between a group of Surinamese Muslims and the municipality of Zwolle. The Surinamese Muslims had established their mosque in an old school building owned by the municipality. The local league of homosexuals had been allotted space in the same building for its regular club meetings. The Muslims wanted the homosexuals expelled.[7]

The situation was complicated by the fact that the Muslims had not paid the rent for their space they had in use since 1981; they hoped to receive a subsidy from the municipality. The municipality informed the Surinamese Muslims by letter that it could not condone what it regarded to be discrimination against the homosexuals. Nevertheless, the municipality eventually decided on practical grounds to provide separate accommodation for the two enraged minorities in different buildings.

The municipality justified its original decision to refuse to expel the homosexuals, as requested by the Muslims, on the grounds that homosexuality was generally tolerated in Dutch society. Two prominent observers of Islam in the Netherlands took the view that such a justification effectively blocked all social change (Shadid and Van Koningsveld, 1986). If Muslims in the Neverthelands had different views on homosexuality from the municipality, it followed that no generally accepted view on homosexuality existed in the Netherlands. In this they may have been right, but one wonders whether these two academics really want to advocate the reintroduction of prejudice against homosexuals as a desirable form of social change brought about by the presence of Muslims in the Netherlands.

However, another problem has to be raised from the viewpoint of Muslim law. Does Muslim law permit Muslims to rent a mosque from a non-Muslim owner like the municipality of Zwolle? There is no doubt that Muslims may buy a building from a non-Muslim owner and change it into a mosque, but renting a building creates a relationship in which independence may be lacking. Such lack of independence may have undesirable results, as the case in Zwolle has shown. In that particular case Muslim specialists in Muslim law had to make a decision, but there exists a distinct possibility that such specialists would declare the renting of a mosque from a non-Muslim owner to be forbidden according to Muslim law.

Is the municipality to blame? It seems certain that it would never have considered, for example, providing accommodation in the same building for both the local league of homosexuals and a local young fundamentalist Christian association. Whatever the case, during a summer in which the Dutch press had little to amuse its readers, this episode received major coverage.

In the mosque the Imam plays a dominant role. For historical reasons, the Dutch legal system has had difficulty in recognizing Muslim 'men of religion' as being on a par with the Protestant and Catholic clergy or with the Rabbis. The influential Dutch Islamologist, Snouck Hurgronje (1857–1936), had effectively argued that Islam knows no clergy, no hierarchical system and no priests. His Dutch intellectual heirs understood this to mean that Islam knows no religious functionaries. Official recognition of Imams as religious functionaries – of great legal consequence in the Dutch system – had to wait until the decision of the Dutch Supreme Court in 1986. This decision went against the advice of most specialists, who had all been pupils of Snouck Hurgronje, or pupils of his pupils.

The recognition of Imams as religious functionaries implied that the Dutch legal system declared itself incompetent to give decisions in conflicts between an Imam and his community. Such conflicts are of a religious nature and Dutch courts are not competent to decide in religious matters. This decision also had other consequences. Although it ended discrimination against the Imams, who now are on an equal footing with their Christian and Jewish counterparts, it also weakened their position. The Imams are usually selected by the authorities in their country of origin and sent to the Netherlands for periods of three or four years. However, they are paid by the members of the community that they serve. In case of a conflict and eventual dismissal from their post, they automatically lose their right of residence, and because of their recognized religious status they have no recourse to the court. In their new situation they are dependent on two masters who may hold different views: their community on the one hand, the Moroccan or Turkish authorities on the other.

One of the duties of the Imam is to read the sermon at the communal Friday prayer. This is a matter which creates a difference of opinion between the Turkish and Moroccan authorities and Dutch Muslims Communities. Are the Imams obliged to read sermons that conform to what the Moroccan or Turkish authorities might wish to prescribe? Would diplomatic pressure on Muslim religious functionaries who preach in the Netherlands violate the Dutch constitution, which guarantees freedom of religion to everyone who resides in the country?

This particular question was posed on 27 February 1985 by a socialist member of the Dutch parliament. Many observers have the impression that the Moroccan authorities especially are inclined to put pressure on its Imams to conform to their directives. Nevertheless, in an extremely short statement the Minister of Foreign Affairs made it known that he was not aware of any such pressure. Interestingly enough, his reply was dated All Fool's Day, 1 April 1985.

The Moroccan Imam of the provincial Dutch town of Alphen is attributed with the cause of an incident that, at the time, had comical dimensions – at least in the eyes of outsiders. Rarely have the mutual misunderstandings about the nature and scope of religion become clearer. This Imam had ruled that a Muslim girl could only go to school if she wore a scarf on her head. The municipality of Alphen did not permit girls to wear a headdress in its schools. During the course of this affair the municipality asked for advice from Professor Jan Brugman, professor of Arabic at Leiden University, as to whether the Koran prescribes girls to wear a headdress. The phrasing of this question is interesting, and significant in order to understand better the Dutch concept of religion. The Dutch people are deeply influenced by the Reformation. One of the most notable and well known principles of early Protestantism is 'By the Scriptures alone', *Sola Scriptura*. In the understanding of many Dutchmen, a religious rule or a religious institution not prescribed by the Holy Scriptures ought not to be part of religion or be considered legitimate. For example, in the battle against the Roman papacy and the Inquisition this rule may have been valuable and have given courage to devout Protestant Christians who risked being burned at the stake. Although the *Sola Scriptura* principle is generally accepted in Protestantism, it has little value for other religions.

In Islam, the rules that govern behaviour are not taken directly from the Islamic holy scripture, the Koran, but from Islamic law, which is based, at least in theory, not only on the Koran, but also on the exemplary example of the Prophet Muhammad. Moreover, the rules of Islamic law are based on analogy and on the general consensus between Muslims and their religious leaders. The precepts of Islam are not solely deduced from the Koran, not even by a Dutch professor of Arabic at Leiden University. These precepts are collected in the handbooks of traditional Muslim law, and only the Muslim professional 'men of religion', the Ulema, can establish these rules and expound upon them.

Nevertheless the professor informed the municipality that the Koran did not prescribe that Muslim women should wear a headdress. This answer backed the municipality, who now forbade all Islamic schoolgirls to wear a headdress during school hours in municipal schools. As far as the answer of the professor is concerned, it may be argued that the Koran (passages 24:31 and 33:59) does prescribe such a headdress but this is beside the point. What does matter is that the fundamental rules of Muslim law (which is based on the Koran and other sources) do lay down exactly which parts of a woman's body must be covered in public. The head is one of these parts. If the municipality had cared to consult an Iman, recognized or not, it would have received the correct answer.

In all religions a gap exists between the fundamental rules prescribed by religious functionaries and their daily practice. Islam is no exception. Not all women in the Islamic world cover their heads. Not all Catholic women refrain from taking the pill, whatever the Pope may preach. Nevertheless, in early 1985 the wearing of a headdress was important to Moroccan Muslim schoolgirls and their fathers. Many of them came originally from rural regions where it was not customary for girls to go out and attend school. Yet Dutch law required them to do so. In order to show that their daughters were still respectable Muslim women, in spite of these dubious journeys to school Moroccan fathers insisted on a headdress, and received support from their Imam.

On 8 February 1985 a socialist member of parliament, who also happened to be a Roman Catholic priest, asked the Minister of Education how he felt about the headdress and the position taken by the Alphen municipality. In the Netherlands, questions asked in parliament are a customary means of rectifying irregularities or errors by lower authorities. On 11 April the Minister answered that 'in general' Dutch municipalities should refrain from attempting to interpret the Koran authoritatively, that the municipal decision had been retracted, and that according to him 'it is not proper in our present society to forbid pupils to wear a headdress'.

Nevertheless, although Islamic and other forms of headdress are now officially permitted, many Moroccan parents in the Netherlands still do not wish their daughters to attend school. In order to avoid being prosecuted for evading the law which prescribes compulsory education, they make use of a flaw in the

system. They simply inform the municipality that their daughters
are staying temporarily in Morocco. Children staying in Morocco
fall outside the competence of the Dutch educational system. Such
children are not obliged to attend Dutch schools and to suffer their
iniquities. Once these girls have passed the obligatory school age,
they return – at least as far as the municipal registers are concerned.
If they did not do so, they would lose their rights to family
reunification.

Family reunification, or to be more precise looking for a
marriage partner in the country of origin, is perhaps sometimes
pursued for economic reasons. Even when the new partner knows
he cannot find a job in the Netherlands, he may nevertheless want
to immigrate. Marriage will give him a legal right of residence, and
it is not difficult for someone who legally resides in the
Netherlands to get social assistance when for whatever reason he
cannot get an income from work.

On the other hand, preference for a Dutch non-Muslim marriage
partner may also have economic grounds. This is, for instance,
demonstrable from the contents of a local Islamic religious
monthly, published in Arabic in Leiden.[8] In its discussion of the
problems of 'marriage in exile', *machâkil al-zawâj fi al-mahjar*,
the monthly explains that 'many young Muslim men marry Western
girls because they wish to receive legal right of residence, *raqbbat
al-husûl alâ al-iqâmah al-qânûniyya*. 'Having legal right of residence', with all the material benefits that it may produce, no doubt
plays an important role in many minds. It cannot be denied that to
many living in the West seems much more attractive materially
than living in the Islamic world.

Nevertheless, when marriage partners are brought in from
Morocco or Turkey, religious reasons may play a role too. Many, if
not most, Muslims regard Western society as sinful and immoral.
Western education taints even the most piously educated Muslim
child. Only a bride, or bridegroom who has not been reared in the
Western world can satisfy the demands that parents-in-law feel they
have to make in order to guarantee their children a happy family
life. Hence, a large number of future spouses are imported from
the countries of origin of the Muslim communities in the
Netherlands.

Consequently, in the year 1990 between 30,000 and 40,000
people immigrated legally to the Netherlands. The estimate[9] for
1991 was 125,000. These immigrants are rarely able to find work,
they do not know Dutch, and they receive social assistance in some

form or another. It does not fall within the competence of a specialist on Islam to judge whether the policy of the Dutch government concerning these groups is adequate. The Dutch general public, as far as it is acquainted with these facts, obviously has its doubts.

In September 1991 Mr F. Bolkestein, a member of parliament, voiced these doubts[10], and provoked intense debate in the press. In spite of other burning national issues that competed for attention[11], the Bolkestein discussion was still very much alive at the beginning of December.[12] In bitter readers' letters several points were made: the Dutch also had the right to preserve 'their own culture and language';[13] and the 'general failure' of Dutch policies were attributed to 'immigrantologists' who, through their insistence on 'politically correct' thinking, had paralysed any attempt to rethink rationally the policy towards immigrants.[14]

It is significant that in one of its replies,[15] to Mr Bolkestein's remarks the Ministry responsible expressed the view that he had not initiated this discussion for electoral reasons. Was the Ministry suggesting that attempting to win votes is reprehensible? It may, however, be safely assumed that Mr Bolkestein opened a debate on a sensitive subject, and in the long run such courage might bring in votes – not an action for censure in a democracy based on elections.

Other aspects of the discussion on Islam in the Netherlands are more reprehensible. In 1990 a publisher in Amsterdam printed a small book entitled *The Downfall of the Netherlands: country of naive fools'.* Its author was a certain Mohamed Rasoel. The penname Mohamed Rasoel hid the identity of a certain Z.M. born in Pakistan. Mr Z.M. lives in the Dutch town of Edam and, according to his lawyer, denies having written the book (Rasoel, 1990).

One Dutch critic characterized the book as 'The Protocols of the Elders of Mecca' (Zaal, 1991). The book predicts a Muslim takeover of the Netherlands, which according to the author would take place in the middle of the next century. Strangely enough, the book contains no information about Islam that would not be known by the average Dutch journalist. If the book had been written by a Muslim author, one would expect it to contain at least some information on Islam or Islamic family life that forms no part of the stock of clichés available to Dutch journalism. Moreover, the publisher of the book had already been involved in an earlier literary mystery.

Nevertheless, in May 1991 the Prosecutor of the Court of Amsterdam demanded a legal investigation into the question whether certain of the author's statements on Islam and the future of Islam in the Netherlands, contravened Dutch laws on religious and racial discrimination. The language of the book has a certain quality, but also it has a certain violence, even in passages which have little or nothing to do with Islam in the Netherlands. On the whole, it looks very much as if a Dutch journalist wanted to air his misgivings about the presence of Muslims in the Netherlands (which is his legal right), but did not have the courage to publish under his own name – which makes his case somewhat doubtful. The Mohamed Rasoel affair seems to have died down for the moment, but nevertheless it illustrates that all is not well in the relationship between the non-Muslim majority and the Muslim minorities.

In the Netherlands, it is widely argued that the integration of the Muslim Mediterranean communities will be advanced when Moroccan and Turkish pupils receive special lessons about their own culture and their own language. One of the assumptions behind this argument originally was that these children would eventually go back to their own countries. Consequently, lessons about heritage language and culture have been given since 1970 as an integral part of the programme of Dutch primary schools.[16] The results have not been encouraging. Moreover, the 'heritage language' of Moroccan children in the Netherlands is rarely classical Arabic, or even one of the forms of Arabic generally spoken in Morocco. Most Moroccan families in the Netherlands come from the rural areas around Nador and Al-Hucema in the north of Morocco. At home they do not speak Arabic, but Berber. Which language should they be taught as their 'own language'? It is perhaps due to pressure from the Moroccan authorities that in the case of Moroccan pupils the Dutch have invariably opted for classical Arabic. In the case of Turkish pupils, the situation is equally doubtful: some of them are not ethnic Turks, but come from Syriac-speaking Christian minorities around Mardin, Arabic-speaking minorities from south-east Turkey, Cerkes minorities, Kurdish minorities, or they are Armenian. With the exception of the Cerkes, many of these minorities within Turkey are only superficially interested in the Turkification of their children by the Dutch educational system. Since a return to Turkey or Morocco is no longer envisaged, the motivation that originally existed behind these 'Heritage Language and Culture' lessons has disappeared. Also, the results and the aims are unclear and/or unsatisfactory. Nevertheless, the system still exists.

The problems posed by the necessary primary education of Muslim children may be finding its own solution in another way. The Dutch system gives religious organizations the right to have their own schools, and to have these schools financed by the state if they conform to certain standards. Since, in certain towns well over half of primary school pupils are Muslim, Muslim primary schools have become a distinct possibility. Several already exist.[17] There can be no doubt that if the Dutch 'pillar' system permits Catholic, Protestant or Jewish schools, Muslim schools should be allowed as well. Parents in the Dutch system have the right to send their children to the school of their choice. Do Muslim primary schools contribute to the emancipation of Muslims, or do they hinder the integration of the Muslims into Dutch society?

In the Dutch system the municipalities have the authority to recognize and subsidize such schools. Many municipalities have been hesitant to grant such recognition, but in the long run the system will not permit them to withold such recognition indefinitely.

Dutch religious organizations have the right of access to radio and television. The Turkish Federation of Islamic Cultural Associations[18] has entrusted the production of Islamic religious broadcasts the Islamic Broadcast Foundation.[19] From October 1986 until October 1989 this Foundation broadcast a programme of fifteen minutes weekly on television and one hour weekly on radio. Since October 1989 the Foundation has half-an-hour weekly on television and two hours weekly on radio. It is not surprising that these programmes reflect the views of Islam which the Turkish authorities prescribe and encourage. The organizational structure of the Islamic television and radio programs once more demonstrates the lack of contact between the different Muslim communities in the Netherlands: the share of Moroccan, Moluccan or Surinamese Muslims in these programmes is still limited.

The Dutch authorities seem to assume that in the long run the Muslims in the Netherlands will develop their own understanding of Islam: a Dutch Islam. This form of Islam, it is generally understood, will fit into Dutch society as we know it today. Perhaps the Rushdie affair demonstrates that this may be true. All the Muslims I have met in the Netherlands declared that Rushdie's *Satanic Verses* should be forbidden, but at the same time they expressed the wish to read the book themselves. Also, as has been pointed out by prominent Dutch Muslims, in spite of demonstrations and public threats against Rushdie, no cases of actual book burning or attacks on bookshops have been reported in the Netherlands.

This may be reassuring, but for a local Dutch understanding of Islam to develop, the different Muslim communities in the Netherlands should have greater contact with each other, and with Dutch society as a whole, than they have at the moment. At present, these communities are still closely linked to their countries of origin. This may be demonstrated by the preference for marriage partners and dependence on religious functionaries from their countries of origin. Another practice that forcefully symbolizes this attitude is the way in which the Turks and Moroccans in the Netherlands bury their dead: usually a funeral in Turkey or Morocco is preferred to interment in the Netherlands.

It is unlikely that under these circumstances they can move intellectually far away from the norms of their countries of origin. Islam in the Netherlands and elsewhere in Europe will be oriented to the developments which take place in Islam worldwide. These developments, however, are difficult to predict. However this may be, the Muslim presence in the Netherlands has forced both the non-Muslim Dutch and the Muslims in the Netherlands to reconsider their own cultural, political and religious identity. This process may be painful and sometimes unpleasant, especially to people who are culturally insecure, but in the long run both groups can only benefit from such reconsideration, reflection, reconstruction and revitalization.

Notes

1. Known as the 'pillar society' or *zuilenmaatschappij*.
2. The Dutch law by which the construction of churches was financially supported at the taxpayer's expense lost its validity in 1975.
3. *Globale Regeling inzake Subsidiering Gebedsruimten 1976*.
4. *Tijdelijke Regeling Subsidiering Gebedsruimten voor Moslims 1981*.
5. Motion Dales/Wiebenga, 1984.
6. Mosques have also been built with financial help from the Middle East.
7. The Koran condemns homosexuality (e.g. 7:(78) 80–(79)81.
8. *Al-Shurûq* (1991), June 25. The Imam of the Leiden Moroccan mosque is a member of the board of editors.

9. Central Bureau for Statistics, quoted in the Volkskrant,
    29 November 1991

10. Volkskrant, 12 September 1991.

11. The Social-Democrat Party, a government party, agreed to
    reduce social benefits and faced internal revolt.
    Labour unions organized strikes against government attempts
    to change the social security system.

12. See (e.g.) the weekly Elsevier, 30 November 1991: 19–23.

13. Volkskrant, 30 September 1991 (Robert van Waning).

14. NRC Handelsblad, 1 October 1991 (Ali Lazrak).

15. Volkskrant, 20 September 1991.

15. ETC, 'Eigen Taal en Cultuur'.

17. In Utrecht, Leiden, Rotterdam, Eindhoven, The Hague and
    elsewhere.

18. Stiching Turks Islamitische Culturele Federatie.

19. Islamitische Omroep Stiching (IOS).

4

ISLAM IN FRANCE: RELIGION, ETHNIC COMMUNITY OR SOCIAL GHETTO?

OLIVER ROY

One should not be overawed either by the rise of the Muslim population in France, the consequence of immigration, or by a new visibility in religious observance (in terms of the mosque or use of the veil), a result of the conviction that there is no question of returning and that therefore the faithful must come to terms with living among Christians or in a secular society. Far from being a rising force, Islam in France has failed to provide itself with truly representative institutions, for the probable reason that, in spite of there being a French Muslim population, there is no Muslim community.

Ethnic, culturalist and religious demands are attributable to a minority, or rather several minorities, themselves unrelated – fundamentalist, urban-zone youth or those employed to lobby. These demands would appear to represent not so much a token of vitality on the part of a burgeoning community that seeks recognition but a phase in the destructuring of immigrant groups, which are losing their initial culture and restructuring themselves round new, multifarious and often contradictory identities. The question is whether these new identities merely express a transitional phase, prior to complete assimilation into French culture, or whether they are the precursor of new forms of community expression that go against French tradition. The answer depends very much on the groups concerned. 'Gallicization', while continuing to observe religious practice on an individual basis, would seem to be the end result of the process of integration for groups which are socially and economically assimilated. On the other hand, a new kind of ethnic identity, a characteristically American kind, which in the place of attachment to a specific national and religious identity takes the form of shared fellowship as a sub-culture within the dominant culture, seems likely to prevail among the young Arabs (and Blacks) of the urban zones, who are casualties of the integration process.

Muslims in France

Muslims in France are mainly of Arab origin, but also include Turks, sub-Saharan Africans, Pakistanis and even French converts. There are three levels of identity concerned, which sometimes intersect but never quite coincide – ethnic identity as defined by place and language of origin (Arabic, Turkish), religious identity (Islam), and nationality as defined by current passport (French, Algerian). Confusion between these three levels renders the debate complex and emotive, but this is inevitable since it reflects similar confusion in the minds of the participants.

Formerly, the term 'French Muslim' referred exclusively to Harkis (Algerian soldiers loyal to France) and their descendants. Now more than 30 per cent of Muslims living in France were born there. The proportion of French citizens among Muslims is increasing, because of immigration controls, naturalization, and the birth and education of children who will automatically acquire French citizenship. The tendency to acquire French nationality is particularly marked among those who originate from the Maghreb (Algeria, Tunisia, Morocco), as opposed to other Muslims – Turks, Pakistanis, those from Mali and so on – who still nourish the myth of eventual return and who, for the time being, show little concern to assimilate. Use of the mother tongue, rejection of intermarriage and strength of community systems of education and interdependence keep such communities alive as well as setting them apart, in spite of internal social discrimination (older members exploiting the newly arrived) and political divisions (among Turks, for instance).

But for those who originate from the Mahgreb, the question of nationality is now separated from the religious question. Within the context of existing legislation, they are becoming and are bound to become increasingly French. The break with the country

of origin is becoming more noticeable (dialectal Arabic is regress-
ing, modern Arabic is a school subject, embassies and social clubs
play a decreasingly visible role). Oddly enough, the political situation in the country of origin arouses less response in the Arab
immigrant population than do more general questions affecting
the Middle East, such as Palestine or the Gulf War.

Unlike earlier waves of European immigration, members of the
second generation of Arab immigrants are perceived as Arabs, as an
'ethnic group', even when they are French citizens and have
French as their sole language. Does this imply the emergence in
France of an American-type manifestation of ethnicity, reinforced
by identification between an ethnic group and a religious (i.e.
Islamic) community, or does it simply point to delay in the
ineluctable process of integration? Behind apparently straightfor-
ward labels there is in fact a high degree of complexity, because
both forms of representation – the ethnic and the religious – are
facing crisis. In France, properly speaking, there exists neither an
Arab community nor an Islamic community in the real sense of the
term, instead there is a withdrawal into their shell of the casualties
of the integration process (i.e. young urban Arabs) and various
strategies to project a sense of community on to a Muslim population which does not see itself as such. These strategies reflect three
forces, which paradoxically converge, in spite of their divergences:

1. Islamic lay preachers, often foreign and connected with
   Islamic international organizations;
2. An élite that is integrated but of immigrant origin, which seeks a
   role as intermediary and interface between a community
   perceived to be more ethnic than religious and the French
   government and French society;
3. The French government, anxious to find groups or individuals
   to negotiate with from a community in crisis and so forestall
   the emergence of a political, allogeneous form of Islam.

However, these forces come up against the same problems: the
weaknesses and divisions of organizational Islam, which make it
difficult to set up a 'French Muslim Church'; different degrees of
cultural integration, making the task of defining a community in
ethnic terms a precarious one; and the reconstitution of social
identity among the young *beurs* (North Africans born in France)
from urban zones (the very ones who are both the *raison d'être*
and target of the three forces) round a subculture of revolt, itself a

product of the dominant culture, indifferent to religion, authenticity and community solidarity.

Muslim population or Islamic community?

In spite of the efforts of missionaries and a few Islamist intellectuals there is no real religious solidarity in the Muslim community in France capable of transcending ethnic, linguistic and national divisions. There are virtually no mosques frequented by both Turks and Arabs. As a rule, whenever it is materially and administratively possible to establish a number of mosques, the pattern will be for one Turkish, one Pakistani and several Arab ones, the dividing line for these being more 'ideological' (fundamentalist as against moderate) than national (Tunisian, Moroccan and so on). Islamic institutions are fragmented, social clubs often rivalling each other; nowhere is there the organized clergy or undisputed leadership capable of imposing religious edicts (*fatwa*).

There exists no overall authority to represent the Islamic community. The Grand Mosque, under the control of an Algerian sheikh, has no institutional authority over the other places of worship and is called into question by the Fédération Nationale des Musulmans de France, itself run by French converts, while a multitude of locally organized Islamic social clubs administer the mosques in urban zones. Islam in France is locally based around a small mosque, usually serving a monoethnic group, or else around a charismatic personality such as an imam; and there is always the tension of divergence between moderate and fundamentalist in the background.

More surprisingly, community feeling is markedly slight among French Muslims, leaving aside the cultural associations that have charge of the mosques. Cultural clubs or places to meet other than mosques (cafés excepted are seldom and there are very few sports and recreational clubs. Privately run Islamic schools are thin on the ground. Clubs where young *Maghrebins* are in the majority (some sports clubs for instance) are never linked to any Islamic or Arab organization. Only the Turks run a series of clubs, but here the exception proves the rule: there is no single Islamic community but a number of ethnic communities, among which the most numerous, comprising those from the Maghreb, is the one least provided for in terms of social clubs and societies.

Why should this be so? First, because probably the will to preserve the identity of the country of origin is simply lacking, since it has no meaning. Second, because the population is not homogeneous but made up of people of different national origins, Moroccans, Tunisians and so on, who are at different stages of assimilation. Third, because there is a divorce between Muslim identity and Arab identity. Muslim activists are opposed to what normally enables an ethnic or national community to safeguard its cultural identity. Music, folk groups, fêtes and dances are frowned on by Islam because of the mixing of the sexes, the threat of dissolute behaviour and of heathenism, or simply their absence of reference in the traditions of the Prophet. 'Fêtes' are confined to the mosque and to the family circle. The community is unable to see itself as such in a public festive setting. Islam refers to the *Umma*, the community of the faithful, and theoretically, especially in fundamentalist circles, refuses to attach any value to ethnicity, nationalism or indeed any form of Arab. culture that may seem to be distinct from Islam. An Arab may see Islam as one component of his identity, but the opposite is not valid.

'Arab' ethnic identity is something experienced passively rather than laid claim to. Nor is it reinforced by Islamic identity. So what about Islamic identity?

Which Islam?

Islam, as it has been codified by the doctors of the law, is an all-embracing religion that defines not merely the sphere of belief, rites and practices that are both individual and collective, but a body of principles that regulate social life. If Islam has always accepted the presence of the other – Christian or Jew – in its midst, orthodox Muslim thought cannot conceive of a minority form of Islam as other than provisional (as Bernard Lewis makes clear in Chapter 1). Yet immigrant Muslim populations do experience life as a minority and will continue to do so; leaving aside the colonial parenthesis, this is a new experience for so large a Muslim population.

For twenty years or so the myth of returning enabled the matter to be shelved. But today French Muslims are having to assimilate the fact of their being in a minority and give it institutional expression.

How then is Islam experienced or reincorporated? First, there is time reserved for individual practice, then for forms of community practice and expression, and here it is not always easy to distinguish between manifestations of Arab-Islamic, not to say Mediterranean, 'culture' and those of a religious community endeavouring to live by its own rules.

At the level of the individual, being Muslim implies observing the five cardinal precepts: profession of faith, the five daily prayers, lawful almsgiving (*zakat*), fasting during Ramadan, and the pilgrimage; added to these, the consumption of certain foods (pork, for instance) is forbidden as is the consumption of alcohol. But the domain of Islamic law (*shari'a*) goes beyond individual observance and governs social behaviour in general; though the implications and the nature of this 'all-pervasiveness' are subject to debate and interpretation in the Muslim population.

How is this reflected in the Muslim population in France? Individual observance is minimal among young people and those who have continued with their studies. The first practices to lapse are the ban on alcohol, insistence on halal food, the five prayers, the *zakat* and the pilgrimage. Minimal observance consists of asserting that one is Muslim, adhering to the principal rites of passage (circumcision, reciting the *fatiha* at the marriage ceremony, and burial), not eating pork, and fasting in Ramadan (for at least three days). The latter is frequently the only individual rite observed by young people and the last to be abandoned.

The degree of theological knowledge is generally negligible. What is perceived as Islam is often an assortment of basic Koranic prescriptions, popular religiosity, folklore and tradition. There are cultural elements too, which have more to do with 'Mediterranean culture' than with Islam: for instance, the exaggerated sense of honour and the supervision of girls by their brothers are an imperfect expression of the prescriptions with regard to morality and modesty, which apply in the *shari'a* to both sexes.

This tenuousness of theological learning is given greater emphasis by the decline of Arabic among younger generations in favour of French. Dialect keeps its place within the family, the vehicle of communication in the group is French; from the outside, classical Arabic, which is taught at school, is seen as a foreign tongue of little value. Finally, the Islamic model for observance competes and clashes with the new subculture developing in urban zones.

Even so there is a sense of attachment to Arab roots, but this finds expression in a sphere pertaining more to ethnic than to religious identity: preserving a sense of identity in one's children (giving a Muslim first name, except in the second generation Harkis), outward respect for Islam, identity with the Arab world (as in the Gulf War), and support for Third World issues in a way that is entirely compatible with recognisable left-wing positions in France. Rather than the Koran, it is history that is called upon and all this amounts to a perception of oneself that is more ethnic than religious.

Ethnic group: experienced as a reality but elusive as a concept

Ethnic group is seen more in terms of a look and of a history than of an ethnically definable reality. Ethnicity does not mean the transfer on to French soil of a community from elsewhere, which has preserved its identity, its rites, its religion, its cooking, its language and its dress, and which demands respect and recognition. Yet some such notion lies behind the bogus debate on what constitutes a community and 'respect for cultures'.

In the so-called Arab 'communities', Arabic is not the vehicle of communication and religion is perceived as having a more symbolic role than one of concrete observance. The traditional, patriarchal family has broken down. The authority of the eldest son often outweighs the father's, while a distinct cultural split divides the generations in regard to music, dress and food. The picture of immigrants reciting prayers on the grass outside a council block and then grilling *merguez*, conversing in Arabic and listening to Um Kalthoum, is a quite mistaken one. Today they go along to McDonalds, listen to rap and speak French. What remains are a few 'festive' observances within the family (the sacrifice of a sheep to mark the end of Ramadan, for example), and the sense, confirmed by the attitude of others, that one is an 'Arab'. The problem for the Muslim population is that the diverse and complex elements of identity, which might go towards developing a sense of community, normally involve a compromise with the dominant culture, a reinvention of what one is that owes nothing to one's place of origin, whether it is a question of Islam, ethnic group or culture in general.

Hence, leaving aside that restricted élite of Muslim origin that has become entirely gallicized, the Muslim immigrant population as a whole can be considered to have adopted a complex cultural register, where facets of adaptation combine with residual attitudes that belong more to the Mediterranean than, properly speaking, Arab culture and in which a corner is kept to express rudimentary notions of Islam where popular custom, superstition and orthodox theology are all confused. The contradiction is clear: for many young Arabs the customs relating to Islam represent a cultural token, occasions for celebration, a folklore; but this conversion of Islam into ethnic terms and into folklore is rejected and attacked by the fundamentalist lay preachers. What the religious militants say contradicts the experience of 'passive' Muslims and hinders the spontaneous fusing of ethnic identity and religious identity.

Thus in France there is a population made up of Arabs and/or Muslims, but there is neither an Arab community nor a Muslim community that seeks to be recognized as such. The problem is one of a community becoming destructured and continuing to have an existence only in the imagination of its members and others. The demand for recognition of a community comes not from the rank and file, but in general as a response to strategies devised elsewhere.

Strategies for community building

I shall single out three strategies:

1. The goal of forming the Arab-Muslim community into a particular interest group, and as such an active factor in French society. What is involved here is integration by means of prior community building, on the basis of an undertaking to show tolerance to the Islamic religion in exchange for its accepting the non-sectarian principle and the private nature of religious observance, this being underpinned by a modernist and moderate interpretation of Islam:
2. The goal of 'grass roots' reconversion of the Islamic community, so severing it from French society while accepting this ghetto condition as an inner form of 'Hijra' (migration), a symbolic and somewhat schizoid means of enduring Islam's position as a minority.
3. The goal of the French government, which is fed by two fears – that the racial issue will become both politicized and socially explosive, on the lines of American-type ghettos.

Can there be a Muslim lobby or interest group?

Today Arab immigration has given rise to an élite that is integrated and that either repudiates any notion of constituting a community and of a 'Muslim Church', or else plays on its success to try to win recognition as an interface between the Arab-Muslim community and the French government. This would imply creating the context for a community on the basis of having achieved integration in effect as an individual. The attitude adopted in regard to Islam is an ambiguous one. This group is made up of people who in general have a non-sectarian view of society, but who agree to lend their weight to demands for Islamization, because such demands help the community to acquire a sense of itself which has been lacking until now (the presence of mosques, authorization to wear the veil).

These 'mediators' are often self-proclaimed or paradoxically designated, or even trained by the French government ('approved and capable figures' organisers and educational experts). Called upon *in extremis* to provide leadership for refractory communities, they convert this emergency function into a business and make use of their government-sponsored legitimization to try with a greater or lesser degree of success to impose themselves on a 'community' which in fact has little interest in who represents it.

This strategy is forestalled by the divisions of the community and by the fact that in the end the ethnic connotation 'Arab' is seen as pejorative and hence seldom laid claim to, except by young *beurs*. In fact the young *beurs* are highly critical of former immigrants who have moved into positions of influence and claim to represent them, but whose self-promotion and inevitable complicity with those in government and politics seem to them suspect.

The greater the degree of integration, the less assertiveness there is about ethnic origin. It is unlikely that an Arab political lobby will make its appearance in France.

Paradoxically, the one factor that produces a relative mobilization among the population of Arab origin has to do with external politics. The Israeli-Palestinian conflict tends in a reflected way and from the outside to set apart the Arabs and Jews in two antagonistic communities, whereas neither in their makeup nor in their social or economic integration do they find themselves in a situation of rivalry, symmetry or even cohabitation.

Grass-roots reconversion to Islam

Another strategy of 'community building' is that which is prevalent among fundamentalists who seek to recreate a purely Islamic community within a society that is seen to be infidel. An alternative society such as this, made up of the uncompromising, rejects any ethnic definition and so excludes 'erring' Muslims, even though the missions particularly target those of Muslim origin. The strategy is one of deliberate rupture, which rejects integration and resolves the problem of the minority position of Islam by negotiating the question of its own autonomy and a special status for what is 'Islamized' with the government. The field of neo-fundamentalist mission is generally non-political. The message it delivers is not that of overturning the state, but eschewal and non-integration.

Hence it is not a case of having to face an influx of traditional Islam. On the contrary, the kind of fundamentalism that is preached in mosques today is in open defiance of the sentimentalist view of religion common in the Maghreb, still mixed with the idolizing of marabouts. The new missionary zeal not only campaigns against popular Islam, the cult of marabouts and of music, but also against mysticism and syncretism, and hence against tolerance. The new militants preach formalism and adherence to the body of scriptural law and tradition and they contest the Islam of philosophers.

The goal is to set up pockets of Islamic observance within society, where the norms one would like to see applied universally preside. Everyday life must adapt to the practice of Islam: time set aside for prayers, halal food, timetable adjustment for Ramadan, the school system conforming to Islam (exemption from physical training and biology classes, separation of sexes, linguistic and cultural propagation of Arabic). The methods applied are those of door-to-door proselytizing and unofficial gatherings. Muslims are targeted where they are vulnerable – guilt over lapsed observance, hopelessness and misery, longing for dignity in a debased world, and hostility to Western values.

The activists of such neo-fundamentalism are more often than not 'born again' Muslims, who are long-term residents and have adapted but not fully integrated. They are usually manual workers or in trade and are stalwarts of cultural circles and clubs, or else lay preachers, who are rarely permanent residents in France but come especially from the Middle East or the Indian subcontinent. Mention should be also made of the role of many teachers of

Arabic (or Turkish), sent over by their respective countries to state schools, and who give instruction in religion and endeavour to counter the integrating function of the school system. Finally there are the French converts, who are active in the National Federation of French Muslims and display the zeal of neophytes.

When the government sets up a community

During the 1980s the French government found itself having to face outbreaks of violence in the urban zones and penetration by Islamic fundamentalism. Since the 1960s administration of immigrants in France had been delegated to their countries of origin, by means of associations linked to embassies, official imams (the Paris mosque) and the secret services of the countries of origin. But with the Muslim community becoming increasingly gallicized, it was inappropriate, to say the least, that it should be administered by foreign powers; the French Muslim community had to be dissociated from the Islamic world in general. Then with the threat of communities forming in the inflammable urban zones, there was the need to find leaders with whom to negotiate.

Although the French government declines to recognize ethnic groups as such, it does recognize religious communities. So by setting up a French Islamic community, the government's hope is to sever the link between Islam in France and its overseas sponsors and to provide itself with an interlocutor.

On this basis the Conseil de Réflexion sur l'Islam en France (CORIF) was set up on 6 March 1990 by Pierre Joxe, Minister of the Interior. The measure is a positive one in the sense that it constitutes an obstacle to the takeover of the mosques by overseas fundamentalist groups, and that it may contribute to a formulation of doctrine appropriate to Islam in France – one which is better able to reconcile Islamic values with a secular society. However, there is a risk of fostering and strengthening community building among Arabs living in France by restoring the links between ethnic group and religion which were starting to crumble. There is a paradox in this treatment of an ethnic community as a religious community by a secular state.

Ethnic ghettos and French sub-culture

Different degrees of integration exist which reflect how and at
what level this is achieved. Today a tenuous form of integration is
illustrated by the young urban-zone *beurs* whose often violent
opposition to society – showing itself in criminality and provoca-
tive behaviour – generates reactive racialism and dismissal on the
part of the rest of the population. The *beurs* conduct themselves
and are perceived as 'Arabs' or *Maghrebins*, yet they portray virtually no sign of Arab culture or the Muslim religion. In fact, by the
very violence of their attitudes, they show a fascination for the society that appears to exclude them. The culture of the urban-zone
beurs has virtually no Islamic constituent. It is a subculture that
functions along the lines of popular culture by pirating the dominant culture. There is a fascination with things modern which are,
so to speak, hijacked and travestied (joyriding with stolen cars, for
instance). Hence rebuilding an identity is based essentially on a
code of behaviour or posturing borrowed piecemeal from the host
society: taste for Chevignon clothes (a name that suggests a Loire
valley wine or cheese from the Auvergne), music, fast food,
language – all of it demolished, stripped down and put together
again, from *verlan* (use of back slang) to break-dancing.
Construction of an ethnic stance is also a form of do-it-yourself.
    The 'Islamic demands' that sometimes emerge from these young
beurs – changing the times of classes during Ramadan, for instance
– are not evidence of reconversion to Islam but rather a form of
deliberate provocation, which is directed particularly at the school
administration and teachers, with little attempt at coherence. For
these youths what matters is not wresting a guarantee of conditions for religious observance in school but an occasion to make a
gesture, not so much to show that they are different, but to make a
gesture of refusal by laying claim to what has been presented for
ten years and more as the greatest threat to France, the presence
and practice of Islam.
    Yet, on the other hand, this modern urban subculture is assimi-
lated and perceived as an American form of ethnic experience.
There is no reference here to the Muslim population as a body.
The troubled urban zones relate to some tens of thousands,
unconnected with the millions of people of Muslim extraction
living in France. The question is to know which of two predictions
is the more likely to come about. One where Muslims who are
assimilated will eventually dissociate themselves from the youth of

the urban zones, whose problems will then be seen as essentially social ones; or one where the emphasis is more ethnic and where the 'rogue' group of urban-zone youth will gradually take on an emblematic role, leading to an 'ethnic' recasting of social relations in a way that goes against French tradition. The attitude of the Maghrebin élite could well provide a key to the problem.

5

ELITES OF MAGHREBIN EXTRACTION IN FRANCE

NADIA RACHEDI

The notion of modern citizenship as something separate from specific identity and distinctive characteristics is an invention of the French Revolution and thereby given political legitimacy. The secular principle, asserted and applied more unequivocally than in other countries, is invested with particular fervour. The separation of public and private – the domain of religion – is an accepted principle of communal life. The French find it literally shocking that, as in Germany, one's religion is a matter to be recorded on an identity card. The teaching of Islam in schools and wages paid to imams by the state, as is the case in Belgium, are against the law in France. Moreover their introduction would fly in the face of people's sense of political legitimacy. The furthest step taken has been to introduce a non-religious body, the Conseil de Réflexion Sur Islam en France (CORIF), to represent Muslims, rather on the model of the council representing French Jews, and to negotiate with the authorities on the question of responding to the specific needs of the Muslim population. The secular principle remains invested with something sacred, which was transferred from the sovereign to the nation by the French Revolution. What might well have appeared to our friends abroad as absurd conflict involving three foreign girls and their Islamic headscarves in a Paris suburban school in October 1989, in fact well exemplified the fundamental link between the secular principle and political legitimacy.

Refusal of ethnic particularity

The denial of the term 'ethnic' in French sociology shows the degree to which sociological thought, for all its pretensions to objectiveness, remains bound to the sense of nationhood among sociologists. If Durkheim like Mauss disallowed the concept of ethnicity, the reason is that it designates a reality opposed to the principle of citizenship – an abstract body of rights and duties, far removed from distinctive identities. But it is not that these are denied, as is too often mistakenly alleged, they are simply consigned to the domain of private concerns and interests; and thereby they escape sociological attention. 'Society', in Durkheims's view, that is to say the French nation, does not acknowledge the existence of ethnic groups in the public arena, it recognizes the right of individuals to declare specific adherences only in their private lives, on condition that their expression is not to the detriment of law and order.

The current debate in France remains between sociologists who advocate 'integration' and those who advocate 'community further-ance', as does the debate on both scientific and ideological ethnic-ity. The conflict has to do both with social reality – are there foreign 'communities' in France? – and with politics – should we now endeavour to integrate people of foreign extraction through the medium of distinctive communities, as being better adapted to modern societies, or should we continue to assimilate people as individuals in the way that the nation-state has traditionally done?

The fact of integration

Until now all sociological studies concur in showing that immi-grant children whose schooling has been in France have become culturally bonded to French society and are determined to become integrated. They have acquired the same knowledge, display the same gaps in their knowledge, the same scholastic and cultural indicators, and they adopt the same attitudes as French children from comparable backgrounds. As Dominique Schnapper (1991) remarks, the somewhat hasty pronouncements made as to the inef-fectiveness of the educational system need qualifying, at least as far as life style and system of values go. Underachievement at school certainly does not have to do with school as a vehicle for socializa-tion; especially since, contrary to a widely held belief, underachievement by immigrant children born in France is only slightly lower than that of French children whose background is similar. In fact it is precisely because they are seen to be culturally integrated that they find it impossible to make common cause on the basis of specific identity. Their involvement in political life is based on principles and practice other than 'ethnic'.

The impossibility of returning to the country of origin – theirs or their parents' – is evidence of the depth of cultural integration. The adoption of urban models and the value system of the country where they live make it difficult, if not impossible, to contemplate going back to a country judged to be 'archaic' or 'mediaeval' in the light of life lived in France. The most commonly held ideology is no longer that of pursuing the 'right to be different', which was gradually abandoned during the 1980s, but has become that of 'integration', however ambiguous the term in a political sense. Even within the Socialist Party and among the Greens, the Third-World-inspired movement for the 'right to be different' is losing ground. In this respect too, changes in young people of Maghrebin extraction are no different from changes elsewhere.

Family customs are gradually falling into line with those of the majority of French people from similar backgrounds. This is borne out by population statistics and in social surveys. The number of marriages between Algerians and French women tripled between 1965 and 1982 and partnerships between Frenchmen and Maghrebin women increased tenfold over the same period, although in the latter case such unions are forbidden by religion and constitute a form of betrayal, thus testifying to the reality of integration, even though statistical procedures based on nationality overestimate the figures. The age of marriage has risen; whereas for Algerian women it was 19.1 on average 20 years ago, it is now 23.9. While fertility still remains higher than for French women, it dropped by half for Algerian women resident in France between 1962 and 1980. Reflecting a general trend in the French population, the practice of cohabitation is making its appearance among young Maghrebins.

The case remains, however, that there are a great many children of immigrants in the depersonalized suburbs of the larger cities, where the disintegration of working-class culture has left a moral and spiritual vacuum. Algerians in particular are over-represented in so-called 'special' schools and in youth unemployment figures, which are particularly high in France. More than other groups, they are linked to petty crime in urban areas. Moreover, their visibility is

raised because social workers, politicians, journalists and sociologists, in their different ways, constantly dwell on it in the
comments they make. There is a further danger that their presence
and the exploitation of xenophobia in the surrounding population
by the *Front national* may one day lead to 'ethnic' conflicts.

In France although the discourse and ideology of the last decade
may have exalted the virtues of distinctive cultures and been critical of the practices of the centralizing state, the actual policies that
have been followed are an extension of traditional attitudes
regarding foreigners established in France – what was previously
described as 'assimilation' is now known as 'integration', which
consists of giving foreigners living in France the means of becoming actively involved in public life and granting them citizenship to
authorize and encourage this involvement.

The Gulf War

The Gulf War provided an occasion to put these analyses to the
test. During the weeks preceding the start of military operations
there was much speculation on the likely reactions of the Muslim
population, in particular those of Maghrebin extraction. Would
their 'Arab' solidarity lead them to demonstrate actively against
French policy, leading perhaps to violent confrontation with other
elements in the population, the Jews in particular? Perhaps one
would see a community type of organization developing among
them led by their élite?

A survey carried out at this time in regard to individual reponses
among the Maghrebin élite during the Gulf War in fact enabled the
hypothesis of such attachment to a policy of 'community
development' to be tested.

Well established citizenship

The majority of individuals who constitute this élite hold French
nationality, either through naturalization, reinstatement or by
virtue of dual *jus sali* for those born on French territory, and they
occupy well qualified positions which characterize them as successful and upwardly mobile. As a general rule, they hold reputable
degrees and are represented in all branches of intellectual and
economic life in France. Their specifically political activity is slight,

most noticeable among those who are younger, were born in France and play a part in local politics. There are in the region of five hundred municipal councillors of Maghrebin extraction, testifying to fairly recent entry into the political arena. For others, although their political engagement was strong at the time of decolonization it fell off considerably and even altogether with the disillusionment that followed, though they continue to vote. They are both highly gallicized and attached to their country of origin, which they visit regularly. Most of them have a partner who is not of Maghrebin extraction as well as children whose first names denote their 'in-between' situation – Loris-Tarek, for instance, or Lisa-Farah, the second name often being a sentimental or symbolic acknowledgement of their native country. Though Muslims, they are in the main non-believers and non-practising. Most of them came over to France alone, frequently with an academic or professional ambition which was influenced (as regards attitude towards going back) by trying economic and political conditions in the home country or by a process of abiding gallicization due to a long time spent in France, making a return problematic.

The survey deals with two population categories: those with direct experience as migrants and those born in France to immigrant workers. If forms of relationship to French society sometimes vary, all have become socially and professionally integrated.

The findings enable one to understand better how such integration has been achieved and to examine ways in which this élite might represent the population of Maghrebin origin. Interviews carried out before the Gulf crisis reveal the individual nature of integration achieved. Those interviewed in no way claim to represent others of Maghrebin stock in France or to have a sense of belonging to a community with its own distinctive culture. They consider themselves to be complete citizens and playing a full part in communal life. Most of them acquired French nationality through a deliberate act of choice, in which both professional considerations (bearing directly on the question of nationality) and adherence to French values played a varying part. They take the view that their position is indistinguishable from that of anyone of French 'stock' of the same generation. Interviews conducted before the war provide an indication of the degree of professional and social integration on the part of a population which has tended to merge as individuals into the French population. Few of them pursue activities linked to their country of origin; their socializing forms a fairly general pattern – sports and recreational clubs, circles made up of friends or linked to business.

The Gulf War made them feel 'pushed aside' 'shut out', and treated like Jews during the Six Day War. They felt that they were suspected of having dual allegiance, both to French society and, via a cultural link based on common ethnic identity, to Iraq. Yet they saw themselves in a quite different light. If the Gulf War made them feel a link with Iraq, shadowy notions of Arab solidarity had less to do with it, they say, than fellow feeling with the Iraqi people based on universal principles. As far as they were concerned the war did not give rise to 'twin loyalties' or call into question their citizenship and involvement in French society:

'I've no emotive ties with the Arab world as has been suggested by the political class. That said, my attitude has been little different from other people's, considering it all as something of a farce, this trying to represent the West as the repository of knowledge, intelligence and power, at the same time wanting to play the role of international policeman on any and every issue.' (Company head, born in 1951 in Nanterre.)

They felt that the French government lumped them together as a 'community', whereas all they wanted was to be seen as individual citizens who had embraced the principle of neutrality and stuck by it. The time when 'citizenship was extolled' and when they had felt treated as fully paid up members of French society gave way to a time when France, being involved in the conflict, questioned their rights as citizens:

'I found it difficult to accept the way the French state looked on us as hostages by addressing the Algerian or Maghrebin or Arab 'community' in France, by addressing Muslims as if the secular principle had no place in the Arab community, whereas previously they'd made such a hoo-ha about it. I've found it all very disturbing, and the way of looking on us as hostages. In fact, I'm very uneasy about the future and the way the whole question of immigration into France is likely to be handled.' (Doctor, born in 1945 in Algeria.)

The term 'hostages' well expresses their experience of the war. And they often make use of other terms such as 'parenthesis' or 'in abeyance' to point out their situation during the Gulf crisis. Such expressions convey their feeling of not having been thought of exclusively as French citizens whereas it was above all as French citizens that they saw themselves and behaved.

'Throughout the war we were half citizens or even part-time citizens.' (Financial adviser, born in 1954 in Tunisia.)

Their feeling of not having been accorded recognition as French citizens went along with a fear of having to face the reappearance of social attitudes similar to those that had been common during the period of decolonization, in particular the protracted one affecting Algeria. History provides a reference in developing memory that is indissolubly both collective and individual. Every society possesses a history, on the basis of which collective memory forms and from which an individual draws the elements that go to make up his or her personal identity. This history acts to cement and safeguard the sum of identities and the collective memory of every society. So it is that in every individual there is a portion of the 'historical unconscious', in other words a part of collective memory that re-emerges when the feeling arises that one's personal identity is threatened. With Jews, the memory of Shoah recurs whenever Jewish identity or Jewish destiny appears to be called into question, a striking example being the Six Day War. Maghrebins had a similar reaction at the time of the Gulf War: a sort of update on the end of the colonial period was instantaneous. There is no need to recall the conditions under which the countries of the Maghreb obtained their independence, but it does need to be emphasized that the fear of seeing a repetition of the scenario was instantly present. The war awakened memories in those who had lived through the wars of independence in the countries of the Maghreb. The fear, as they put it, of again becoming 'victims' by association in the eyes of French society forced them to behave with extreme prudence as long as the conflict lasted.

The Gulf War similarly produced repercussions both at work and in everyday life:

'My parents-in-law are Jewish, and what if while I'm having a meal with them at 8.30 there isn't a scud missile attack on Jerusalem, while the Elysée takes the opportunity offered by the 8 o'clock news to bring up the Holocaust, and people are putting on gas masks in Jerusalem with the alert sounding in Tel Aviv – all this is going on, and there I am and I have to say something. I make it clear that a Jew is as good as an Arab and that with all this happening you've got to continue to believe in democracy.... With my father-in-law we keep our cool, we argue bitterly but there's no violence, we don't come to blows. In fact you couldn't have a more explosive subject than that. Put a Jew and an Arab together, however much they may like each other, there's something somewhere that sets them off; so if you get on to that topic, you have to keep a tight hold on what you're saying and know when to stop.' (Company head, born in 1959 in Nanterre.)

In the opinion of those interviewed, by identifying the Muslim population with the 'potential enemy', French society betrayed its fear that the situation would get out of hand and could lead to active conflict between sections of the population. They remarked that the media were the first to talk about the 'mass purchase of handguns in the southern regions of France' following the declaration of war on Iraq, at the same time mentioning that seasonal workers from Corsica were heading back to the Maghreb. In their view there was little doubt that France was getting ready for a civil war. All the time they exercised strict control on everything they said:

'There are a lot of people I've talked with and also a lot I haven't talked with. Those who I knew held extremist views and didn't understand a thing. Those too who harangued me simply because I was North African. So I preferred to forget it.' (Actor, born in 1952 in Oran.)

Throughout the crisis what they said in public was very different from what they said in private, thus showing they knew how to abide by the rules whereby conflicts between individuals and groups can find a voice under French democracy. The Gulf crisis constituted a test of their membership of French society, a test imposed, in their view, by the others.

Those held responsible

Journalists were accused of being initially responsible for the feeling of not being recognized as French citizens, but as 'Arabs' maintaining specific cultural links with Iraq. Journalists lumped together 'Arabs', 'Muslims', 'Iraqis' and 'Maghrebins' and confused those engaged in the Gulf conflict with those who were resident in France, 'with whom attempts have been made to establish community or religious links':

'Added to this we've been much abused in the media. A semantic shift occurred in no time – moving from Saddam to dictator, dictator to Arab, Arab to criminal and so on. I've never had any illusions about the media. I've worked with them and 70% at least of the people there are totally ignorant. There's been no solid, deeply researched documentary about Iraq. Iraq has simply been turned into the enemy to be destroyed, and along with Iraq Arabs,' (Journalist, born in 1950 in Morocco.)

Politicians were also held to be responsible, together with intellectuals as a body, including Jewish intellectuals whose 'extremism', it was felt, was given tolerance in a way that would be refused to 'Arabs':

'Today I can't ever forget the intransigence shown by French Jewish intellectuals, which I find quite inadmissible. Their comments on television ... Just imagine a second-generation North African saying a tenth of what G. said or others have got away with. The violence used is quite exceptional, you just can't use this or that resolution to justify massacring the whole Iraqi nation.' (Company head, born in 1959 in Nanterre.)

'What I couldn't accept was the position adopted by French intellectuals who were conspicuous either by their absence at the many and different demonstrations or by their official line of simply sitting on the fence.' (Director, born in 1951 in Nanterre.)

They reproach the political and intellectual class in French society with failing to clarify an already complex situation, especially with abdicating the chance of any real debate. They see themselves as the 'victims' of generalizations deliberately cultivated by intellectuals and politicians.

A new relationship with the state and citizenship?

Their testimony makes it clear that they felt they were being made to undergo an ordeal in the course of which they had to take control of themselves so as not to respond to the image which, they felt, French society was trying its best to thrust upon them. But they also felt that it gave them a chance to display their attachment to democratic values.

In this respect, the result of the Gulf crisis was to bring into being a new type of rapport with politics in France. For some, 'France acted in the only way possible'. They were in total agreement with the French government and its entry into the war alongside the USA. They showed their disapproval of the extremism evident from pictures taken in countries they were born in – 'First and foremost, I'm French'. They frequently claimed to defend the French government. During the conflict, for instance, they levelled criticism not at French policies but at those of the USA, which in their view were responsible for the war:

'The Americans have far more to answer for, claiming to police the world
as they do, it's they who started this war and brought in several other
countries, including France. It's well known that Bush was head of the FBI
and the fact that they came into the war with such speed is linked to
special interests they needed to defend in Kuwait. Because, as everyone
knows, Kuwait is no more democratic than Iraq.' (Company head, born in
1952 in Algeria.)

Those in agreement with the French government were in the
majority, given that they represented a significant number in a
limited and qualitatively defined sample. For others, disagreement
with the French position led to a change in their vote:

'I shan't forget that period in my life. I mean it'll take a lot for me to go
out and vote for the Socialist Party. Indeed I'd be inclined at the next elections to tell young *beurs* – and plug it properly – not to forget a government that's acted like that. I agree with Régis Debray when he said that
socialist France feels the need at regular intervals to go out and do an
Arab. He meant it in another sense but it's true; Mitterrand enjoys doing
an Arab or two.' (Barrister, born in 1926 in Algeria.)

'I say that Mitterrand is scum, but that's well known, it's nothing new.
Mitterrand conducts foreign policy just as he does home policy. With us
he's never been any different, when he boosted the Front national to
make our lives a misery, it certainly doesn't make our everyday life any
easier, a strategist is how he thinks of himself and so he plays around with
people's lives. He's more or less the same in international dealings, he's
someone who plays rather cynical politics.' (Company head, born in 1957
in Algeria.)

With their perception of being a French citizen damaged, and
disappointed by the attitude of a government for which most of
them had voted, they nonetheless upheld their status to a man:
'More than ever we remain fully citizens, ready to protest but citizens all the same.'

Lastly, there are those who were against the position of the
French government and who supported the Iraqi people, and
sometimes Saddam Hussein. There were two instances in the
sample taken. They see Saddam Hussein as the agent of a modern
world and the first to assert Arab identity in the face of the West.
They identify with him as a hero on account of their own anti-
Americanism, which encourages them to rally to his side (though
they are well aware of how he has treated his own people and the
Kurds), and on account of the non-religious nature of his regime.

Vaguely they yearn for some form of public recognition for Arabs and their distinctiveness within French society, but without openly calling for the creation of a community:

'I'm for Saddam Hussein, with my heart but not my mind. Why? I don't know, I mean I know when he gassed the Kurds it wasn't something the media acclimatized us to. We see Saddam Hussein as the victim of American imperialism, also in some sense the Iraqi people are close to the Algerian people, both are strongly attracted to the secular idea, at the same time the Algerians are a proud people who have fought to defend themselves. I think the identification goes a long way.... I'm not of course explaining the gut feeling that draws me to Saddam Hussein, while I know quite well he's a fascist, in public I say that I condemn the invasion of Kuwait but in fact I don't give a damn, I'm not concerned by what he did to the Kuwaitis, frankly I don't give a damn.' (Company head, born in 1957 in Algeria.)

For them Saddam Hussein is the incarnation and living affirmation of an 'Arab' public identity through which 'Arabness', with its distinctive characteristics, can find acceptance in the Western world. Yet while they demand the particularity of 'Arabness', they refrain from advocating communities and, above all, they don't question the principle of citizenship.

The Gulf War precipitated a 'crisis' insofar as it reflected an image of an 'Arab community' on to a population which perceived itself exclusively as made up of citizens. Never for a moment was the principle of citizenship called into question. Opinions about French policy did no more than produce shifts of a partisan nature.

The question that remains is the following one. Has the mere fact of focusing on an 'Arab community' brought it into being? Even if the Gulf War obliged the most gallicized of those of Maghrebin extraction to reformulate their identity, choice of citizenship has been unanimous. For some individuals the war aroused both conscience and resolve to restore the sense of a shared 'Arab' cultural legacy. Nevertheless, the 'Six Month' war was probably too short to enable them to become organized and encourage the élites to come forward as mediators and leaders. The lack of any direct intervention on the part of such leaders showed that they were not willing to offer themselves as representatives of an 'Arab community' whose existence they have never accepted. When they analysed their position vis-à-vis Iraq and the countries at war they did so with reference to international law, hence in universal terms. The war failed to set off any particular demand for identity. Being 'too gallicized' and integrated both professionally and socially, they were not tempted to reformulate a new identity, which combined 'Arab identity' with membership of French society. The Gulf crisis had the principal effect of mobilizing them on the issue of universal rights, not on that of distinctive identity. Some of them became aware of the lack of organization and representation among the population of Maghrebin origin. Attempts to deal with the problem were made, often by circles that had existed before the war, but there was no move towards becoming organized on a collective basis. Clearly the pattern of individual integration is set.

Above all the crisis revealed the degree of attachment to France among the more prominent members of the Maghrebin population and the non-existence of 'dual loyalty'. In the words of a barrister:

'It is to be hoped that after this long and awkward silence common sense will return. Let it be understood once and for all that not the slightest doubt remains as to our loyalty and our total adherence to the French Republic and its institutions.'

6

THE POLITICAL CONTEXT OF MUSLIM COMMUNITIES' PARTICIPATION IN BRITISH SOCIETY

CHARLES HUSBAND

My aim is to provide a brief account of the political context within which, in contemporary Britain, Muslim communities are seeking to negotiate their citizenship and their ethnic identities. While the Muslim population of Britain is made up of a wide range of national and ethnic groups – some coming as immigrants, others as refugees, the predominating groups are those originating from the Indian sub-continent: from Pakistan and Bangladesh. It is in relation to these 'Asian' Muslim communities that I shall develop the following discussion.

While Muslims were resident in England in the seventeenth and eighteenth centuries in small numbers, the major settlement of Muslim immigrants in Britain occurred with the post-World War II influx of labour to fuel the British economy. Since they came to fill a vacuum in the indigenous labour supply these migrant workers became highly localized around specific industries and in specific conurbations.

By the late 1950s popular resentment and racist political factions began to create an increasingly vociferous opposition to immigrant settlement and in 1962 the Conservative government introduced the first Commonwealth Immigration Act to placate these sentiments. Through the 1960s and 1970s there was political capitulation to these racist sentiments, as each party sought to demonstrate its greater rigour in controlling 'coloured immigration'. The sequence of Immigration Acts associated with this process brought to an end the pattern of chain migration that had characterized the early years of immigration, and created the conditions in which the permanent settlement of ethnic minority communities was inevitable. Increasingly families came to join their kin and ethnic communities, often closely mirroring village and community networks in the Indian sub-continent, became established in British inner cities. The majority of these people and their children are now British citizens. Their presence provides one catalyst for contemporary discourse concerning the definition of Britain's national role, and British identity.

National and European discourse on identity

In Britain today an Anglocentric Britishness is mobilized self consciously and ubiquitously by a range of hegemonic interests. Central to the neo-Conservative politics of the Thatcher era, it has also been more subtly modulated through the less orchestrated, though socially significant efforts of a distressed intelligentsia's efforts to come to terms with the external reality of Britain's changing international standing, and the internal calamities consequent upon major structural changes in the British economy.

Within this contemporary negotiation of a hegemonic British identity there is an historically available repertoire of imagery and stereotype, which locates Islam and Muslims as alien to British life and culture. This history is relevant to our understanding of how it could be that the 'Paki-bashing' of the 1970s was essentially anti-Asian, while the response to Khomeini, the Rushdie affair and the Gulf War have contained highly salient anti-Islamic elements. What I wish to suggest is that historically derived stereotypes of Islam and 'the Orient' are continuously latent within British popular culture and learning.

William Montgomery Watt (1991) points to elements of this imagery in the mediaeval European Christian response to Islam, which he summarizes under four headings:

1. Islam is false and a deliberate perversion of the truth (e.g that while some of what Muhammad said was true, it was mixed with falsehood and deception).
2. Islam is a religion that spreads by violence and the sword: an implication of this view was that while Christianity was a religion of peace, which won converts through persuasion, Islam was proselytized through violence and threat.

3. Islam is a religion of self-indulgence: particularly this invoked notions of sexual excess, and unreliability in other matters.
4 Muhammad is the Anti-Christ – since Muhammad had set himself up to create a religion in opposition to Christianity he must be an agent of the Devil.

Watt suggests that these distorted images of Islam, which were formed by Christian scholars in the twelfth and thirteenth centuries, still inform certain strands of European thought today. Added to this, Saïd (1979) argues that as an academic and intellectual field of study 'Orientalism' has, since the nineteenth century, contributed to articulating European identity through defining its other in the 'Orient'.

Both authors identify the moral and cultural otherness of a non-Christian geographical space, and recognize in it threats of polluting difference and of actual physical threat. We have here an illumination of the historical processes underlying contemporary conceptions of European identity. The essence of Saïd's analysis is to identify the means whereby colonial Europe constructed its projected alter-ego in a geographically defined, alien domain. This interplay of theological and geographical boundaries has allowed for confusion, and a negative *bricolage* of imagery in the production of English stereotypes of specific ethnic minority groups. Thus English representations of events in the Iran of Khomeini, and in the Gulf War have been unambiguously detached from their geography and translated into the popular imagery of Islamic fundamentalism as a feature of the British Pakistani communities. The Rushdie affair, and specifically Ayatollah Khomeini's *fatwa*, of course provided a linking of 'oriental political pathology' to 'Islamic fanaticism'. Its effect was magnified by the crassly xenophobic television coverage of Iran and the Iran-Iraq war and by the subsequent demonization of Saddam Hussein and the coverage of the Gulf War. However, in order to understand adequately the response to these events, we must first place them and the Muslim communities in the context of the last decade of British politics.

Identity, 'race' and nation – the Thatcher years

Thatcherism had a profound and probably irrevocable effect upon the economic base of British capital and amplified structural changes in Britain that have impinged upon Western European capital in general. The traditional foundation of the British economy in the manufacturing industry was savaged by closure and internationalization of ownership. Consequently, the centre of gravity of the British economy and the class system shifted to reflect the preponderant interest of finance capital. The social upheavals which accompanied this process have been character-ized by high unemployment, the first wave disproportionately affecting the working class, and the second the middle class and professionals.

In pursuing a strident liberal philosophy of achieving 'the mini-mal state', Thatcherism in fact oversaw an unprecedented central-ization of political power, and the accelerated development of what one major review called 'the coercive state'. This process led to the erosion of the powers of local government and the comple-mentary concentration of power in central government; major incursions into civil liberties, including new constraints on free-dom of speech and an extension of police powers; attempts to increase political controls over the broadcast media, and the selec-tive appointment of politically 'sound' senior civil servants.

These economic policies had a severe effect upon large sections of the ethnic minority Muslim communities in Britain. Given their demographic profile, their skewed class distribution and concen-tration in specific vulnerable industries, they have been particularly hit by unemployment. Given their class and age profile and family structure, they have been very vulnerable to the consequences of the government assault upon the welfare state. Central govern-ment limits on local authority expenditure in particular aborted programmes from which they might have collectively benefited. The high profile inner-city programmes which followed the riots of 1981 did not compensate for the net loss of funding to ethnic minority communities occasioned by these government limits. The Pakistani and Bangladeshi communities have also suffered the effects of an equivalent ideological assault.

The New Right

The Thatcherite political programme was not only underpinned by neo-liberal economic policies, but also drew heavily upon neo-conservative philosophies. These stemmed from Burkean Thought and involved a strong sense of tradition, expressed in relation to the continuity of language, religion, political structures and common culture. This tradition was seen as best expressed in an unashamed sense of national consciousness, protected by a strong state apparatus.

It may seem that there is a contradiction between the minimal state of neo-liberalism and the strong interventionist state of neo-conservatism. Within Thatcherism this was not so. The social upheaval generated by the neo-liberal economic and social policies necessitated strong government intervention to coerce compliance. In order to guarantee the conditions under which a free market can operate, strong government intervention was required. At the same time a strong state required legitimation and the mystical nationalism of neo-conservatism provided a supportive ideology.

The populist rhetoric of Thatcherism has been examined by many political analysts who have, for example, stressed the interweaving of ideologies of nation and family, of nation and 'race', and the concern to establish links between public, state and national identity. Within this project the neo-conservative tradition is fundamental in seeking to evoke a national sentiment which transcends the divisions of class. However, given the race theory that is inherent in this historically rooted national sentiment, race is not transcended; rather it is intrinsically linked with the concept of nation. This mythic fusion of race and national identity was classically summarised in Enoch Powell's 1968 statement that: 'The West Indian or Asian does not, by being born in England, become an Englishman.'

Since 1968 the articulation of a racialized conception of nation and national identity has been heavily influenced by what has been characterized as the new racism. The power of this new racism lies in its dissociation from Darwinian scientific racism and its Nazi associations, and its capacity to see self-interest in a multitude of manifestations as 'natural'. In this way linkage between the ideologies of family, nation and 'race' is established in the natural and indeed inevitable preference for 'one's own'. From this it follows that the 'genuine fears' of responsible people that their family, nation or 'race' may be disadvantaged in relation to 'outsiders' becomes almost a virtue. The new racism, like possessive individualism, makes self-interest normal.

It is difficult to exaggerate the extent to which 'race' and nation have been fused in the last decade of British politics. New right political discourse has presented ethnic minority communities settled in Britain as an 'enemy within'. Ethnic minority communities as a whole, or particular segments such as ethnic minority male youth or 'Islamic fundamentalists', are presented as involved in activities which are a threat to the social order and political stability. Indeed it is as 'threats' to the imagined cultural, political and religious homogeneity of white British society that Asian Muslim communities in Britain are routinely discussed.

The discourse and politics around the 'enemy within' has of course taken place in relation to a parallel debate focused on the enemy without. With primary migration virtually at a standstill, it has been the threat of new immigrant sources – refugees and Hong Kong – and the political threat to British sovereignty – Europe, which has from different directions fuelled the same concern with defending national identity and national borders.

While the 'new Europe' constitutes a cultural and political threat to neo-conservative ideologues like Norman Tebbit and Nicholas Ridley, the bureaucratic processes already underway are ironically drawing upon a vision of Europe that shares their xenophobia, constituting a threat to British ethnic minorities. These fictions of Europe are found within the border policy of the EC, particularly in relation to citizens from 'third countries', where the perceived threat from 'the South' has achieved crisis proportions. These assumed common interests of European cultural identity are also found in the European Community's 'Television Without Frontiers' Directive, where the odious subversion of alien cultural influences must be resisted. For Britons, European identity is potentially merely another annulus in the circles of membership that share common mythic iconography. For ethnic minority Britons 'European' may represent an extension of the field of exclusionary politics, which characterizes their marginalized minority status.

The current political context

The discussion above has attempted to provide the reader with a brief sketch of the wider political context within which Muslim communities exist in Britain. In essence I have pointed to the impossibility of isolating immigration and border policy from internal minority policy. Thus through the 1960s and 1970s it was immigration legislation which converted migrant populations into settled minority communities. The political discourse around this immigration legislation also provided the major platform for rehearsing English racial identity and facilitated the growth of popular racism and neo-fascist extremist parties. The 'respectable' parliamentary parties moved over to the right as they sought to contain the successes of the 'extremists'. Similar processes are apparent in contemporary France. Thus, settled Asian Muslim communities have developed in England during a period in which 'race' has been a recurrent issue in party politics.

These same three decades have seen a transition in the British definition of citizen from one which, prior to the immigration legislation of 1968, was based on a common allegiance to the monarch and which approximated to Heckmann's demotic-unitarian nation state (Chapter 8). The vast majority of settled Asian Muslims have British citizenship, which they acquired through laws and institutional practices derived from the heritage of the British Commonwealth. Now they practise these rights of citizenship in a much changed legal and political climate. Successive Immigration Acts, culminating in the Nationality Act of 1981, have moved Britain toward Heckmann's ethnic nation state. The ideology of English ethnicity currently permeates strongly the dominant political discourse of citizenship.

Paradoxically, Britain is also a *de facto* multi-ethnic society, which through its Race Relations Acts of 1968 and 1976 has actively recognized this reality and made formal institutional attempts to promote 'harmonious community relations'. In this sense it is unlike Germany; but equally in terms of the minimal resources committed to this task it is unlike the Netherlands of the last two decades. In Britain, unlike France, ethnicity and ethnic minorities are formally recognized in data collection, in institutional statistics of the state and in private industry. Equal employment policies are widely advocated and variably implemented. The rhetoric of multicultural tolerance in Britain that informs elements of government policy is also criticized by a broad range of commentators from within the left of the dominant white society as well as from activists in the minority communities. Such criticism points to the continuing widespread manifestations of racism in British life; and to different policy goals which arise from a commitment to justice and equality rather than to tolerance.

Mulsim communities in Britain and the party political system

A simple translation of indigenous British class notions on to an understanding of the political participation of Muslim communities

in Britain is untenable. There are many cross-cutting variables of
nationality, ethnicity, past background, current residence and
work, and denominational commitment within Islam that fracture
any notion of a homogeneous Muslim community in Britain.
Indeed it has been said that the only thing to have united Muslim
communities within Britain has been the Rushdie affair.

There is a cumulative body of research on the relation of 'Asians'
to the British political system, a great part of which is associated
with the work of Professor Muhammad Anwar. Much of this is of a
psephological nature, tracing the electoral behaviour of conglom-
erate categories of 'Asians', 'Afro-Caribbeans' and 'Whites'.
Referring to the extent to which members of Asian ethnic minorities ensure that they are on the electoral register Anwar notes that:

The reasons for non-registration include the newness, the language difficulty that Asians and some ethnic groups face, the general alienation of
some groups, and feared harassment and racial attacks from the National
Front and other such organisations, who could identify Asians from their
names on the register. There is also the fear of 'fishing expeditions' by
immigration authorities. Finally, it could be the administrative inefficiency
of the Registration offices (Anwar, 1990, p. 304).

To this list we might add the effects of the Conservative switching
of local taxes from rates levied on house values to a poll tax levied
on each person in the house. This was associated with the sudden
loss of huge numbers of people from the electoral register, as
households with a number of residents found their tax bills had
increased dramatically.

Given their demographic location it is apparent that 'Asian'
communities in British cities have access to potential political
leverage since, at the level of the ward in local council elections
and the constituency in parliamentary elections, their votes may
now be critical. On the other hand, because of the absence of
proportional representation in the British electoral system the
national impact of 'an Islamic vote' may be minimalized, but in
specific constituencies their support cannot be ignored, nor
increasingly be taken for granted. Thus, for example, the
Conservative party has an 'ethnic minority unit' within their
Central Office's Department of Community Affairs whose function
has been, since 1976, to make party members conscious of the
importance of the 'Asia' and 'Afro-Caribbean' vote, and to influence party policy to improve its image among ethnic minorities.
Similarly the Labour party has a Black and Asian Advisory

Committee, which has comparable functions. Although wishing to attract the 'Asian' vote, both the Conservative and Labour party have been reluctant to advance ethnic minority participation in the House of Commons.

While the Conservative party has advanced a coded but unmistakable form of racial nationalism, it should not be assumed that the Labour party reflects a pristine celebration of the equality of all within what is left of its socialist ideology. This is the party which introduced the discriminatory and racist 1968 Immigration Bill, and in recent years it has been careful to sustain its 'strong' position on immigration issues. In addition, the Labour party would not submit to strong pressure from Black groups to overcome its resistance to the introduction of Black sections.

Anwar (1990) provides a telling synopsis of the history of the selection of ethnic minority persons to stand as parliamentary candidates which may be summarized in the following manner:

- In 1970 there were three ethnic minority candidates who stood for the Liberal party.
- In February 1974 the Labour party and the Liberal party each put forward a candidate, neither with a chance of winning.
- In October 1974 there was only one ethnic minority candidate, for the Liberal party.
- In the 1979 General Election, one Labour candidate, two Liberal and one Conservative: they contested seats they had no chance of winning.
- In 1983 there were 18 ethnic minority candidates representing 4 parties, only one of them contesting a marginally winnable seat, which he did not win.
- In the 1987 General Election there were 27 ethnic minority candidates, 4 of whom were elected.

The treatment that some of these candidates received in the British national press during the 1987 election campaign and subsequently was a telling indicator of the normalization of racist sentiments within British political discourse.

The 'Asian' communities in Britain, with one elected MP, Keith Vaz (Leicester East), have still much to achieve in converting their demographic and electoral concentration into parliamentary representation. However, the evidence is that these communities are increasingly and variably mobilizing to increase their impact upon party politics in Britain.

Their potential impact at the local level may be illustrated by LeLohe's study of the 'Asian' vote in Bradford, of whom sixty per cent are Pakistani. He summarizes the situation thus:

To have a council which swings between the two major parties and which has most of its seats classified as marginal is unusual. It is also a situation in which the votes of particular groups, if organised and located in the marginal wards, could be so crucial as to give such groups considerable power. The Asian communities are certainly well-organised to exercise their voting power. Indeed the Conservative Leader in the Council stated that they were well aware that research showed Asians were twice as likely to turn out to vote in council elections as white voters (LeLohe, 1990, p. 66).

LeLohe demonstrates how efficient the 'Asian' leadership within the Labour Party at ward level has been in mobilizing the Asian vote. Indeed in Bradford there has been a vigorous penetration of the Labour party structure by a coterie of relatively young 'Asian' professionals; some of them having made the transition from young community 'radicals' to well-placed local authority bureaucrats. Interestingly, in a parliamentary by-election in Bradford North in the autumn of 1990, a candidate for the Islamic Party of Britain gained only 800 votes in a seat won by the Labour party with 18,619 votes. On that occasion the Council of Mosques in Bradford, which had attained national visibility following its high profile in the Rushdie affair, remained neutral and gave no advice to Muslim voters.

It is indicative of the power of the Muslim community in Bradford that they are somewhat over-represented among the Labour councillors on the local council. However, this power is not without its ambiguity for the Labour party. LeLohe's analysis of elections in local wards shows the 'white' Labour voter to be 'sensitive' to their candidates' 'race':

The Asian communities at both Heaton and Keighley were consistent, just as diligent in voting in 1983, 1984, 1986 and 1987. The problem was not the Asian voters, it was the whites and their prejudices about Asian candidates. The Labour candidates in Heaton in 1982 and 1983 were Asians and they had helped build up the Asian vote. When they stood down for a white candidate the Asians still voted Labour and their votes elected the winner. The reverse sadly does not apply for, in non-central Bradford, white voters display a prejudice against Asian candidates.... Labour lost Odsal in 1987, which has an overwhelmingly white electorate, in 1987 with Shah Khokhar as the candidate and in 1988, despite the support of the sizeable Asian community Shankat Ahmed lost the supposedly safe Labour seat of Undercliffe (LeLohe, 1990, p. 74).

To complement the above psephological perspective upon Muslim community party political behaviour I now add two brief 'case studies'.

Islam as a physical presence: discourses of dominant resistance

Here I draw heavily on the work of John Eade (1991) who provides a splendid case study of the sensitivity of indigenous English values and interests to the Islamic presence in England. Eade shows how the physical manifestation of an Islamic presence may be problematized and politicized within discourses apparently far removed from that of theology and 'race'.

Tower Hamlets was until recently a predominantly working-class area of London, associated with labour dependent upon the nearby docks. The area has a long history of immigrant settlement, ranging from Calvinist Huguenot silk weavers in the seventeenth century, Irish Catholics in the eighteenth and early nineteenth century, Russian and Polish Jews at the end of the nineteenth century and, more recently, immigrants from Malta, Cyprus, the Caribbean, Somalia and Bangladesh. The latter represent twenty per cent of the population, and are much the largest minority community in the borough. In some wards of the borough they represent between thirty and fifty per cent of the population.

This vignette is important to an understanding of the analysis which Eade develops, for it is clear that we are not speaking here of a pristine, white middle-class enclave. On the contrary Tower Hamlets is an essentially multi-ethnic working-class area with a long history of immigrant settlement which is now experiencing economic and demographic change due to a rapid expansion of office development and the gradual 'gentrification' of conservation areas by wealthy owner-occupiers.

Eade (1991) explores the response to the Bangladeshi communities' development and use of two mosques. One, the East London Mosque, was moved in 1985 to purpose-built accommodation on Whitechapel Road, constructed in a distinctive 'Oriental' style. The other, the Brick Lane Great Mosque occupies an eighteenth-century building, constructed by the Huguenots, which is listed as a 'building of architectural and historical interest'.

The Brick Lane Great Mosque and the conservationist lobby

The issue raised in the conflict ensuing between the Brick Lane Great Mosque and the conservationist lobby is the right of lawful owners, operating within local planning regulations, to alter the physical fabric of the interior of their property. The property in this case happening to be a Georgian Huguenot building, which had previously served as a Methodist Chapel, and as a base for an ultra-Orthodox Jewish society, the Machkizei Hadath. Following a visit by General Ershad in 1985, the Bangladeshi government had provided money for the construction of a new floor, which would accommodate a further 600 worshippers. This essential work to meet the evident need of the Islamic worshippers required the destruction of the galleries and pews that overlooked the ground floor of the old chapel. No change to the external fabric of the building was required or intended, nor was planning permission required. However, vociferous opposition to the intended work arose from the locally influential Spitalfields Historic Buildings Trust, and in particular from one of its committee members, Mr Dan Cruickshank, an architectural historian and the features editor of the national weekly *Architects' Journal*.

Given the rich immigrant history of the area and of this building, it takes a specific reading of the locality to see this 'Georgian' fabric as part of an indigenous culture. While we may recognize the values expressed in preserving historical buildings, we may also note the instances when these values are evoked and the interests they currently represent. In this case Eade points to the link between the conservationist lobby and the conflict of interest between the current immigrant, working-class population and the gentrification of the area. Since no change to the external fabric of the building was proposed, we may legitimately speculate as to what demand for access to the interior of the building by non-Muslims was anticipated by the conservationists. Years of neglect seem easily negotiable when 'cultural alien forces' threaten dominant interests.

The political process of constructing a consensual understanding of a shared physical, national and communal fabric is brilliantly analysed in Patrick Wright's *On Living in an Old Country* (1985). In his account of the interest and imagery, which have been combined to construct and sustain a mythicized 'indivisible heritage' for what he happily calls 'Deep England', we are provided with a broader understanding of the context within which conservationist politics encounter 'alien communities' in urban Britain. In the context of the end of empire, the ambiguous position of Britain among the major players on the world stage, and the marginal position of Britain in the European community, the certitudes of a shared and valued physical heritage is a significant national anchor point.

This brief account, like the next, illustrates how apparently 'neutral' agendas, in this case conservationism, may be powerful vehicles for a *deracialized* assault upon an ethnic group. The particular strength of such a discourse is that while it codes 'race' into the discourse of difference it avoids making explicit the racial agenda.

Halal meals in school – negotiating difference[1]

The provision of halal meals in British schools has focused upon the provision of halal meat. From the Muslim communities' perspective this has been because of concern that their children were unable to eat the meat provided in school meals, for which they had paid. From the perspective of a variety of interests in the white, 'Christian' communities the provision of halal meat was an issue because of the requirement for ritual slaughter of the animal. This raised an outcry from animal rights interests, and from those who expressed a cultural revulsion at the introduction of 'unnecessary and outlandish practices'.

A brief anecdotal account of the introduction of halal meals into one local education authority's schools illuminates something of the political interests involved. The town in question has a population of approximately 20,000 Muslims, the majority of whom are from the state of Gujarat in India and who are residentially concentrated in particular parts of the town. There are five Muslim schools, which have not been recognized by the local authority, and have therefore not been given Voluntary Aided Status by the government. There are also approximately ninety mosques, an Islamic Community Centre and only one Muslim councillor sitting on the local council. Rather belatedly, the Council adopted an Equal Opportunities policy in 1985. Other comparable local authorities adopted such policies rather more rapidly following the 'race riots' of 1981. This Equal Opportunities policy, with the legislative backing of Section 71 of the Race Relations Act, provided a framework in which halal meals could be introduced into the authority's schools.

Resistance to the policy came publicly and vociferously from animal rights campaigners who demonstrated outside the town hall and disrupted a number of council meetings. They also organized a petition, collecting signatures in the street. Members of the Muslim community argued that many of those signing were registering an objection to their culture and religion, rather than to ritual slaughter *per se*. Indeed the animal rights campaigners were accused of being used as a front by racist neo-fascists, and this would certainly have been consistent with the extremists' known strategy. Further, there were letters from all over Britain to the local press urging the council not to introduce halal meat. Occurring as this did in 1989, with the furore in the region and nationally over the 'Rushdie affair', much of the anti-halal rhetoric made possible an easy slippage from the argument that ritual slaughter was barbaric to the implicit corollary that Muslims were barbaric.

We might wonder why, given such opposition, did the council vote to introduce halal meat in the autumn of 1989. One factor was indeed the Rushdie affair; press portrayal of 'Islamic fanaticism' and elite statements from government ministers in which Muslims were reprimanded for their ambiguous Britishness, had given the Muslim community a high profile in local politics. There was a 'moral panic' about the volatility of the Muslim population and they were temporarily a high priority in council considerations. It was at this time that Muslim community leaders close to the Labour party on the local council took the opportune step of informing the Labour councillors that if the demands of the Muslim community were not met then there was a possibility that they would put up an independent candidate in Labour wards where there was a Muslim majority. This threatening suggestion was not likely to be ignored by the Labour party who were in a marginal position.

In addition at national level, the 1988 Education Reform Act provided further threats to the council. This Act, which was a vehicle for promoting the nationalist cultural agenda of the Tory party, amongst other things, asserted the primacy of Christianity in school collective worship. Not surprisingly, this was seen as a threat by many in the Muslim community and they exercised their right to withdraw their children from school assembly. However, the Act also allowed schools to opt out of local authority control and there were a number of schools with a majority of Muslim pupils. This could then have provided a vehicle for the Muslim community in effect to control a state-funded school, something the council had always blocked in relation to Voluntary Aided Status. Given pressures like these, in the words of one observer the council made 'a strategic decision' to introduce halal meat.

Conclusion

The aggregate efforts of local authorities, while showing some undeniable and commendable successes in providing equality outcomes, have failed to make a significant dent in the level of disadvantage experienced by many black and other ethnic minority people. The evidence of continued racism and sustained racial discrimination suggest that the Race Relations Act and a decade of local authority positive action programmes have not significantly reduced the level of race inequality in British society or within local government (Ouseley, 1990, p. 135).

Verdicts such as this have a very real relevance for the political strategies available to Muslim ethnic minority communities in Britain. Particularly they raise questions about what may be expected of the community 'professionals' who have successfully penetrated the bureaucracies of local government in some cities. Given the apparent failure of the democratic political process adequately to respond to the needs of ethnic minority communities, such conclusions point to one of the reasons why cultural struggles will remain an important feature of ethnic minority politics: for, whether it be *bhangra* music or Koranic schooling, there are cultural resources which to a significant extent are outside 'white' systems of control.

Let us briefly examine these questions a little more fully. Participatory democracy in Britain has in this century seen local government as an important political space in which a degree of political autonomy could allow for a response to local circumstances. Over the last three decades this political structure has been a site of policy formulation and implementation, as both central and local government sought to respond to Britain's multi-ethnic reality. This response has moved from a *laissez-faire* philosophy of assimilation in the 1960s to an ambiguous multiculturalism in the 1970s, supplemented by an equally ambiguous equal opportunities philosophy in the 1980s. In some major cities the cultural pluralism that underpinned multicultural politics was replaced by a more radical anti-racist philosophy, which confronted structural inequalities rather than merely negotiating cultural difference. An impetus for such anti-racist strategies was provided by the 'race riots' of 1981, which resulted in a number of local authorities sensing the urgency of recognising the consequences of marginalizing ethnic minority communities. Such was the impetus within a number of 'high-profile' authorities that by 1986 one study (Ben-Tovim *et al*) had published an optimistic account of the possibilities of local organizations committed to racial equality successfully manipulating the politics in the local situation. However, for the new right anti-racism became a focal symbol of the politics of the 'enemy within', and the 1980s were marked by an orchestrated and virulent *anti*-anti-racism. It is difficult to convey the vehemence of the political assault upon anti-racism, and in particular the lurid propagandizing of the press. Furthermore, the Conservative government launched a major onslaught upon local government, and, through the 1988 Local Government Act, outlawed affirmative action strategies for racial equality in mainland Britain, measures which the same government had introduced into Northern Ireland through the 1989 Fair Employment (Northern Ireland) Act, which itself offers rigorous anti-discriminatory protection, on the grounds of religion, to the Catholic community.

Thus, the evidence at present is that while the presence of increasing numbers of 'Asian' politicians and community groups within the local political system may ensure that ethnic minority interests are not totally ignored, their ability to carry sensitization through to policy, and subsequently through to practice, is currently highly circumscribed by the political climate, central government intervention, institutional racism and bureaucratic inertia. Consequently, the factionalism within Muslim communities in Britain, and the conflicting forces operating upon and within local government, incline one to a pessimistic view of the short-term possibility of the political process meaningfully enfranchising the Muslim electorate. National and local party politics will remain a necessary area of engagement for Muslim communities; but it is likely to be a site of struggle which will enhance their sense of marginalization, rather than of incorporation into British political life.

Within the larger context of participation in and membership of British society Muslim communities have, in recent years, been uniquely problematized. So 'successful' has been the new right assault on anti-racism that there is now a popular sentiment that it is the rights of the majority 'white' population that are threatened by 'race relations zealots' and the rapacious ethnic minority communities. Nor has this sense of threat been confined to issues of employment or state benefits; British culture has itself been identified as being at risk. Nowhere has this been more sharply focused than in the élite and popular discourse which has surrounded the Rushdie affair.

The affair has generated a literature of its own and there is no space here to go into detail, but the outrage felt within Muslim communities and the manner of its expression, elicited incomprehension and ethnocentric abuse from a wide range of 'white British' opinion. For those on the right it proved the validity of their 'new racist' arguments. The liberal intelligentsia were fixated by the issue of freedom of speech and censorship, and failed to respond sensitively to the concerns expressed by Muslim spokespersons.

As one partisan commentator has expressed it:

Instead of asking, compassionately, why reasonable men and women can be so outraged by the written work, leading articles even by otherwise thoughtful writers simply condemned the Muslims as Fascists and literary hooligans. Instead of asking why Muslims resorted to such desperate measures, the Liberal Inquisition turned its full fury on a powerless minority. After the Rushdie episode, Muslims are likely to harbour permanent doubts about the fairness and compassion of the liberal conscience (Akhtar, 1989, p. 44).

Clearly the Rushdie affair has been a major catalyst in changing the interface between Muslims in Britain, the 'white' majority and even other ethnic minorities. It has become commonplace for political and sociological commentators to point to the important, but usually unspecifiable, impact of the Rushdie affair. The fact that it was followed by the Gulf War could only have amplified its impact; for the Muslim communities were put under sustained media scrutiny to articulate their relationship to 'the British position'. As the 'enemy within' it did not help their popular image to have to problematize the British conception of the issues and point to Britain's historic role in constructing the geopolitical framework for conflict in the Middle East. As a resident in Bradford I have become used to seeing the town televisually constructed as 'alien', with selective shots of the only mosque with a typically 'oriental' golden dome, and of women with their faces veiled, in order to 'contextualize' an interview with a Muslim community leader.

Given the demonstrable limits of the political process to respond to adequately to Muslim community concerns, and the exclusionary discourses of racialized nationalism, it is not surprising that culture has become highly salient as a terrain of struggle. Education has been one site for this struggle where dietary needs, proprieties of dress, sex segregation and language have all featured in particular communities' attempts to protect their religious and ethnic identity. These demands have been vehemently resisted by the new right as being a challenge to British educational values and indicative of the marginal relation of ethnic minorities to mainstream British values.

Given the concentrated urban location of a large proportion of Muslims in Britain, they have been able to build the commercial and social infrastructure that has enabled them to sustain community languages, dietary provision and such cultural provision as complementary, non-Western, medicine and their own media. The media in fact represent an area of positive success with a diverse ethnic minority press and an increasingly viable range of ethnic minority radio, both legal and pirate. In addition, video television technology in particular, has been exploited in a culturally creative way to meet specific community needs and compensate for the largely monocultural nature of British television. In youth culture too *bhangra* has provided an acceptable musical idiom which, in conjunction with single sex discos, has provided a creative addition to community life. 'Asian' theatre and dance have also begun to achieve a wider distribution and audience. The arts and the media have a commercial viability that allows them a degree of autonomy from the state systems and at the same time to be a vehicle for expressing the heterogeneity, and the common interest, of Muslim communities in Britain.

Cultures of resistance, however, need not be entirely pacific in their operation and the riots of 1981 and 1985 have demonstrated the apparent potency of one mode of political expression. The racial assaults against 'Asian' communities and the unfulfilled promise of the 1980s equal opportunies policies contribute to a sense of vulnerability and grievance which can be politicized. We should remember that in Bradford 'Asians' arrested in possession of petrol bombs were successfully defended in court; their slogan was 'self defence is no offence'. Extra-parliamentary collective action is a part of the contemporary urban scene, and it cannot be assumed that, in the future sections of the 'Asian' communities may not be drawn to it. Certainly the police in Britain are concerned at that possibility.

The Muslim communities in Britain are established now as a de facto part of the social structure of a multiethnic Britain. Much of the difficulty they face in the 1990s arises from the contemporary, hegemonic struggle around the definition of British national identity, and the politics which are derived from this. A defensive boundary maintenance through cultural self-definition is one feature of their contemporary situation. But the heterogeneity of wealth, age, gender and other factors within these communities is reflected in the variety of dynamic initiatives that they have developed. Their demographic concentration provides not only a basis for potential electoral power, but also allows for the social infrastructure of cultural and commercial institutions which provide the structural framework for their continued ethnic vitality. The majority 'white' society's capacity to accommodate to that strength is, in the short term, more problematic.

Note

1. I would like to thank Muhammad Saleem for permission to draw upon his unpublished research in this section.

7

ISLAMIC RADICALISM AND THE GULF WAR: LAY PREACHERS AND POLITICAL DISSENT AMONG BRITISH PAKISTANIS

PNINA WERBNER

Introduction

There are about one million Muslims living today in Britain. Out of these about 400,000 are Pakistanis, originating mainly from the Punjab. Manchester, a large northern provincial commercial city, has about 20,000 British Pakistanis, including their children born in Britain, resident in the city itself and in its southern, more afflu- ent suburbs. They constitute a relatively prosperous community, including many professionals (accountants, solicitors, doctors, engineers), manufacturers (mainly of clothing and knitwear), and small businessmen (shopkeepers, market traders, restaurant and hotel owners, taxi owners/drivers, property rental landlords). There are a few larger businessmen, mainly clothing or food wholesalers and importers. Pakistani businesses employ fellow Pakistanis and women as workers or machinists. At the same time, the community also suffers from high levels of unemployment, especially among older men who lost their jobs when factories closed down in the city and its vicinity. Many of the younger gener- ation are students, studying in colleges and university, while some have started their own small businesses or joined family firms.

Pakistani community politics in Manchester focus around the Central Mosque, an impressive, architect–designed structure, built by the community during the 1970s through internal fund raising, and thus a corporate property governed by a democratically elected management committee. There are also a large number of smaller, sectarian-based mosques in the city, as well as a Pakistani community centre funded by the state, and a plethora of Pakistani voluntary organizations.

British Pakistanis, like the rest of the South Asian community in Britain, have achieved an unparalleled level of cultural and institutional completeness. They have dozens of ethnic food stores selling spicy foods and halal meat, as well as video, music, jewellery, and traditional clothing shops. They run many afternoon and Sunday Koran teaching schools, cultural societies and women's groups. They are currently fighting for the right to establish separate state-funded, Muslim schools, especially for girls. They have their own TV and radio programmes. All these achievements have been made within in a national context where the state provides very secure citizenship and has fostered a relatively *laissez-faire* approach to cultural difference, which is tolerated and even supported by funding for cultural activities, as long as these do not infringe the law.

Although the British Muslim community has suffered from high levels of unemployment during economic recessions, and from racial harassment and discrimination, it is nevertheless a law-abiding community. Until the Rushdie affair erupted at the beginning of 1989, it had kept a very low political profile, preferring to consolidate internal communal institutions rather than fight external political battles. This changed with the publication of *The Satanic Verses*. The protests against the book and the demands that it should be banned have met with very little success. They have sharpened the image of Muslims as irrational and fanatical in the eyes of many ordinary English people, even those who sympathize with Muslims' objections to the book. Their inability to have the British blasphemy laws extended to Islam has underlined for local Pakistanis their political impotence and their sense of alienation, and it is in this context that their response to the Gulf crisis has to be understood.

The Gulf Crisis

In September 1990 I returned to Manchester to find Saddam Hussein, the President of Iraq, firmly established as a public hero among Mancunian Pakistanis. The more Western politicians denounced his bestial monstrosity, the more British Pakistanis extolled his courage, his strength and the justice of his cause. 'But,'

I asked, 'don't you care about the Kuwaitis?'

'Not really,' my most moderate friends replied, 'They are Muslims. What difference does it make who their ruler is?'

'But,' I wondered, 'Are you not concerned that Saddam might invade Saudi Arabia, take over Mecca Sharif and the holy Ka'ba?'

They merely shrugged their shoulders: 'He won't do it,' they said. 'And anyway,' they implied, 'Even if he did, he's still a Muslim.'

Talk of breaking international law and defying the UN charter by gobbling up a member state were regarded with the utmost cynicism. What about Kashmir? And Palestine? Where has UN justice been in relation to those countries?

'But,' I ventured, 'He is a tyrant. There is no democracy in Iraq.'

'Yes,' they conceded, 'Democracy is a good thing. There should be democracy. But tell me this,' they added, 'Which is the greater evil, America or Saddam Hussein?'

Above all they stressed that the dispute was a private Muslim conflict, which should be settled by the Muslim nations without outside interference. They appeared to attach no significance or value to national divisions within the Arab world, regarding them as superficial and insignificant.

What struck me most forcefully, however, even in these early conversations with moderate non-activists, was that once again, as in the Rushdie affair, British Pakistanis seemed to be setting themselves morally apart from the wider society, denying categorically what local people would regard as axiomatic moral imperatives: 'Our boys' were in the Gulf, risking their lives, threatened by chemical warfare, poised to fight the fourth largest army in the world, to defend democratic values against a man who, at the very least, was a ruthless dictator who had invaded and taken over another country.

There were, of course, arguments in the wider society about the tactical advisability of going to war and the heavy costs this would entail. Many thought sanctions should be given a chance. Many doubted the sincerity of the West and saw the war as having purely economic aims. There was an underlying isolationist tendency: why go to war with possible disastrous ecological consequences and terrible loss of life on a matter that was not our direct responsibility? The strong if small British peace movement was quite vocal. Had local Pakistanis merely supported this movement (which they passively did), the English would have sympathized with them. As fellow Muslims, their desire to see a peaceful solution to the dispute would have appeared morally commendable.

But British Pakistanis were not simply talking of tactics, ecology or the potential loss of life. They expressed no sorrow or concern for 'our boys' in the Gulf, nor did they express horror at Saddam Hussein's tyranny. Instead, they spoke of Christian soldiers desecrating the holy ground of the Hijaz, of a Western mediaeval crusader revival, of *jihad*, conspiracy and Western aggression. Thus, they placed themselves almost entirely outside the broad moral consensus, which encompassed both war and peace movements.

This confrontational posture raises difficult sociological questions about the origins of communalism, seen as an ethnic-cum-religious movement. To what extent are such movements inspired by material or political interests, as is sometimes implied in the sociological literature? If such interests do exist, how are we to interpret and uncover them? What type of interests are they, and to what groups precisely do they refer?

On the face of it, the political stance of British Pakistanis struck against their most basic interests as a minority in Britain. Yet what was surprising was their almost naïve lack of awareness that this was indeed the case. Later, as murmurs started in the press about British Muslims being a fifth column, as mosques were daubed with graffiti, as racist attacks on Asians increased (irrespective of whether they were Muslims), some of the more moderate local Pakistani community leaders tried to suppress the most vocal expressions of support for Saddam Hussein. Yet at an all-Muslim conference in Bradford to which the national press were invited, the majority of participants voted in support of the Iraqi leader.

British Pakistanis could have supported the Arab regimes, including Pakistan, which were members of the international alliance. They could simply have kept their heads down and remained entirely neutral. Both strategies would have suited their interests as a local ethnic-cum-religious group. Instead, the majority chose to take a publicly pro-Iraqi stance. Seen from the outside, even the most liberal members of the wider society could only interpret this stance as further evidence of Pakistanis' fundamental irrationality. For the less charitable the stance bordered on treason.

It is worth pointing out, however, that there was nothing illegal in the British Muslim stand on the Gulf crisis – members of the community were perfectly entitled to hold deviant political views; it was just that these views seemed so out of touch with the social environment in which they were articulated.

Let me begin this analysis of the roots of British Pakistani political dissent with a political meeting held in Manchester in October 1990 as part of the *eid-milad-un-nabi* celebrations, a meeting which took place in the shadow of the Gulf crisis.

The meeting

In the corridors of Manchester Town Hall, an ornate, pseudo-Gothic, Victorian edifice, Granada Television is shooting an episode of 'Coronation Street', the local, working-class soap opera. I arrive as Muslim leaders and their supporters begin to gather in the City Council Chambers for their annual Eid meeting. The *maulvi*, the head cleric of the Central Jamia Mosque is there already, a charismatic figure with a black flowing beard and piercing eyes, smartly dressed in black, a fur hat on his head and a green shawl draping his shoulders. Beside him on the podium is an English Muslim convert, a large red-haired man, a local polytechnic lecturer, his huge bulk ensconced in a grey *shalwar-qamiz*. Also present is the *maulvi*'s trusted ally and right-hand man, a local old-timer and radical community spokesman, neat and dapper, his sharp goatee beard is an outer expression, perhaps, of its owner's political acumen. Among the invited guest speakers is a Muslim academic from a northern city, while the proceedings are chaired by a relatively nondescript member of the current Jamia management committee. The committee is entirely dominated at present by the *maulvi* and his radical ally.

Around the hall are large banners in English, held aloft by young boys. The banners, which will later be carried in a *julus*, a religious procession, through the streets of Manchester to the Central Mosque, bear in English a series of religious and political messages: ISLAM MEANS PEACE AND SUBMISSION TO THE ALMIGHTY GOD; ALL MAIN RELIGIONS IN THE UK SHOULD BE GIVEN LEGAL PROTECTION; THE BLASPHEMY LAW SHOULD BE EXTENDED TO ISLAM AND ALL OTHER MAIN RELIGIONS; OUR MESSAGE IS PEACE AND LOVE FOR EVERYONE; MUSLIMS ARE PEACE-LOVING AND LAW-ABIDING CITIZENS; WE LOVE ISLAM AND THE PROPHET OF ISLAM; THE HOLY PROPHET IS MERCY FOR ALL WORLDS. The banners make implicit references to the Rushdie affair through the demand for a change in the blasphemy laws, while asserting that Islam is a religion of peace, and thus rejecting the association of Muslims with violence, which the Rushdie affair has generated in the public mind.

The Council Chambers fill slowly. The Town Hall, ornate, pompous and resplendent, has always seemed an incongruous setting for the gatherings of pious Muslims who use it regularly for their meetings. Built by wealthy Victorian burghers, it was once a symbol of Manchester's manufacturing and commercial wealth. Currently, however, it is dominated by a left-wing Labour council. The history of the city echoes through these incongruities, but the irony is lost on the present congregation. They use the chambers in order to enhance their prestige and that of their group within the Pakistani and Muslim community in the city. Nevertheless, the speakers' rhetoric at the meeting is perhaps not so out of place as it superficially seems. As we shall see, they are there to challenge the established political order, and in doing so they are in fact following a long tradition of radical dissent in the city.

On this occasion, groups have come from all over Britain to celebrate the procession organized by the *maulvi*, who is a key member of their Sufi order in Manchester – the first deputy or *khalifa*, vicegerent, of the saintly head of the order, Pir Abdul Qadr Gilani, based in Walthamstow, London. Significantly, as I later discover, I am the only non-Muslim and the only European present, with the exception of the Muslim convert. Nevertheless, most of the speeches are in English and address the major issues of the day. None of the usual MPs, councillors and invited public notables who regularly dignify such gatherings with their presence are there. Their absence is explained by the fact that the previous year, at a similar meeting in the same chambers, a speaker and the whole congregation had called for death to Rushdie, in the presence of the Bishop of Manchester and a prominent Labour MP, and in front of national TV cameras and the press. This had provoked a furore and a police investigation, which was subsequently dropped.

Purity and dissent

The foundation texts of English working-class dissent, it has been argued, were as much Bunyan's *Pilgrim's Progress*, as Paine's *The Rights of Man*. One of the striking aspects of the speech of Muhammad Haroun, the Englishman and recent convert to Islam, who was first to speak after the opening prayer and sermon by the *maulvi*, was its language, which echoed the familiar cadences of traditional English dissent. Dr Haroun opened his speech with a prayer in Arabic and a general introduction about *eid-milad-un-nabi*. From the start of his speech, he stressed that Islam is a religion of change (i.e. of reform). He immediately went on to explain the kind of change he has in mind:

And this world, Islam says, must be changed to end all oppression. All men and women, Islam says, must be treated with respect and dignity. There must be no inequality, no injustice, no exploitation, no brutality, but all men and women must be brothers and sisters, part of a Muslim nation and part of a Muslim state. Islam is the belief in Allah, but it is also a belief in a unique type of society. A unique social structure. The Prophet was sinless and perfect, he was Allah's instrument to transform mankind [the audience murmurs its approval] and change the world.

Here then is the visionary depiction of an Islamic utopia translated into the familiar language of human rights and equality. At the same time, he attacked the corruption of the secular West: alcohol, greed and materialism are set against Islamic spirituality, love and purity.

Just as English radical movements had their demons and demonology, so does Islamic radicalism have its satans, with the USA and the West perceived as the external source of corruption and evil. On the whole, however, despite mild references to the triviality of English television (all silly stories, drinking and boozing), the first speaker drew his inspiration more from Paine than Bunyan. The demonology of the West and its media is a far darker theme in the speeches that follow.

Western demons and the media

The second speaker began by arguing that 'Islam is not like a scarf on the head; it is like the colour of the blood running through all the parts of the body'. He went on to stress a recurrent theme: the media present distorted images of the Islamic world, lies and propaganda, concocted for a Western audience. This complete lack of trust in the veracity and independence of the media means that even the most public 'facts', such as the plight of the Kurdish refugees, are taken by Pakistanis to represent something other than their obvious meaning for a Western audience. The fundamental rejection of Western news coverage goes along with alternative interpretations of the same events and a mobilizing of a different set of facts. The speaker condemned the sham and hypocrisy of

Western claims to be following 'international law'. Like others at the meeting, he evoked the problems of Kashmir and Palestine, but he also denounced the whole international system, the very structure of the United Nations, which he regarded as biased and based on unjustifiable inequality. In his own words:

This international law that you talk about, this United Nations that you talk about, is just like an angel which is beating its golden wings but is producing nothing. Where was the United Nations in Kashmir, when, in 1948, we were stopped by India from following the will of the people there? ... You come and tell us that we must try to respect the law. We respect God's law, we respect the law of the land where we go, we respect the law of the land where we are born, we are law-respecting people. You preach, you teach, you do not practise. These Bushes, the sooner they are burnt, the better; these Thatchers, the sooner the thatched roof goes, the better it will be, change will come. You can fool people for a short time but you cannot fool them all the time.... What is this double standard? How do you dare talk about international law? I tell you – international law is only a little juggler's trick, it is only a magician's trick.

In speaking of Palestine, Kashmir and Afghanistan, the speaker expressed the direct identification of the present congregation with Muslims in different parts of the world. Islam is a universal, transnational ideology, and Muslims are concerned with the affairs of Muslims living beyond the narrow limits of their immediate community. What we see then in the diasporic politics of the British Pakistani community is a globalizing of local politics, a politics in which the local and the global are inextricably intertwined. What the Gulf crisis has underlined, according to this speaker, is global injustice. And the reason for this is not hard to seek – sheer economic greed. Thus he continues:

The real question is not international law – the real question is oil, it is economic considerations, it is the access they want in order to ensure that their own interests are protected – the West wants to protects its own interests.

But worse still, American greed is matched by the greed of the Gulf states' leaders. These Muslim autocratic corrupt regimes created by colonialism have made a pact with Bush. The external, corrupting evil influence has made a deal with the internally corrupt. The West, however, has failed and is crumbling from within.

In this speech, the configuration of the new populist Islamic radicalism takes shape. The 'ordinary people' are extolled. They form a worldwide community. The corrupt, spineless regimes of the oil-rich Gulf states are merely Western creations – Islam accords them no legitimacy. Was the Prophet a king? And if he, the most supreme of all human beings, was not a king, is anyone else entitled to claim kingship? The target of all the speeches is a single target: inequality. Inequality between nations and inequality within nations. Oddly enough, however, this advocacy of equality goes along with membership of a movement which recognizes an essential inequality: just as the Prophet was the most supreme of all prophets, so too among the living and dead there are saints (*awliya*), who are intrinsically superior to run-of-the-mill, 'ordinary' human beings.

Is this a contradiction? What it exposes is that we are not dealing simply with Paine and the radicalism of the enlightenment, but with Bunyan's quest as well. Kings are intrinsically inferior to pure men of God. Hence God's message of equality is the supreme message and its carriers, holy men, are superior to any amir or sheikh, however powerful and wealthy. The places of these holy men, the shrines where they are buried, are places of supreme sanctity for the congregation gathered at the meeting – all followers of Muslim saints.

Why has Saddam Hussein, himself a corrupt, ruthless dictator, escaped the infamy of the Gulf-state rulers? Is Iraq itself not a Western creation? Partly, as I show below, the opposition to the Gulf-state rulers is a sectarian opposition to the Wahabbi movement. But the main reason Saddam is praised is because he dared to challenge the West directly, and to question the old colonial divisions forced upon the Arab world. For the battle is not only a battle about power, oil and money; it is, above all, a cultural confrontation – a battle for cultural supremacy – almost, even, a battle between the idols of Western materialism and the Muslim all-powerful God. Here the speaker moves from the international scene to the local, British scene:

Now Western culture feels threatened. Look here, these Muslims in Britain, we thought they would slowly dissolve into British society just as sugar mixes with milk, and then they will all be gone. But look at them – they talk like Muslims, they look like Muslims, they behave like Muslims, they respect their parents, they respect their family, they work for longer hours, they are not behaving [like others]; they don't drink alcohol, they do not go gambling.

Once again we come back to familiar, non-conformist, puritanical values: respect for authority, family norms, hard work, abstinence, frugality.

So the English find that these Muslims are a strange sort of people – they had been expecting us to become assimilated but we [Muslims] will not disrespect our faith, our culture.

I work alongside English people. I respect them. But I do not allow them to interfere in those areas which are the areas defined by the Koran and by the *sunna* of the Prophet Muhammad.

My daughters, my sons, my wife, my family, my neighbours, my town, all these people I regulate with the light which comes to me from studying the life of Muhammad Rasul Allah.

So the real crux of the Gulf situation is that there is a cultural conflict between the West and the Muslim world today. They think through their media. The media are playing a tremendous role....

But in the end I would like to say that it is most unfair that in the name of international law you should stop food, you should stop medicine for the Iraqi people, you should try to class people into categories. I am against the Saudi rulers and all the people in positions of power who do not believe. We look towards the Ka'ba and *masjid el nabwi* [the mosque where the Prophet is buried in Medina], Mecca *muazma* [the great] and Medina *munarwa* [the light] with respect. The people who rule over those places should not look towards Washington and New York with the same sort of loyalty. Loyalty ultimately belongs to God, and I say that there should be justice, there should be equality, there should be understanding, there should be humanity. The Gulf crisis will undergo changes; God continually makes changes, and we too must change ourselves. [Here the speaker quotes a verse from the Koran and translates it into English]: God does not change any nation or people unless that nation changes itself.

This powerful speech shows how closely British Muslims identify their particular cause – the promotion of Islam in Britain in order to preserve an Islamic identity for future generations – with the global cause of Muslims. Similarly, the fight against religious legal discrimination in Britain is seen as an extension of a broader, international fight against Western domination. To overcome this domination and internal decadence the community must first change itself, a central tenet of Islamic Modernists. In this fight the national divisions within the Arab world are regarded as a major weakness exploited by the West. The divisions are artificial, colonial inventions; the rulers of these Arab nations are mere colonial puppets. By implication, the solution would be to create a new, unified Islamic empire, which would be powerful enough to meet the West on its own grounds. At this time, in October 1990, British

Pakistanis are still hoping that Saddam Hussein is the man to achieve this power and unity, with his powerful army and intransigent stance against the West.

The final speaker at the meeting, a veteran of many radical meetings, was asked to speak specifically on British issues affecting the Muslim community. He first attacked the illegitimacy of the rulers of the Gulf states and Saudi Arabia, and the complicity of the West and summed this up:

So I congratulate Saddam Hussein for taking the action he has taken. Probably the timing is not right, but it has definitely brought the attention of the rest of the world to an important issue. The important issue that faces the Muslim world. They say that the world is divided, that the Islamic world is divided. It is divided only in one respect. The Muslims of the world today are not divided. They support Iraq. They support Palestine and the people of Kashmir. The ruling families consist of only a handful of people, maybe one hundred, maybe two hundred people. Their security depends on American imperialism and on the Bushes and the Thatchers. These are the people who are on one side and the Islamic world is on the other side.

Once again 'ordinary' Muslims, including the Muslims of Britain, are seen to be the true Muslims, pitched against their false leaders. The speaker moves on to a specific discussion of British Muslims and to an attack on the collaboration between a religious establishment and corrupt exploitative state. Thus radical Islam attacks Muslims' own quietist tendencies and the upper echelons of its clergy. The Saudis, an external, corrupting influence upon British Muslims, are undermining the unity of the community in Britain.

Now the speaker, like those before him, goes on to attack the media. More clearly than the others, however, he expresses a widely held view of a conspiracy:

As regards the problems that are facing the Muslim community in this country – we are a growing community and we are continuously being misrepresented in the British media. We are being misrepresented like this in the British media because the effects of the Crusades, although hundreds of years ago, still persist in the Christian psyche [this theme has emerged since the Rushdie affair]. We are misrepresented because, by and large, the media in this country are controlled by Jewish and Zionist forces. Therefore we will not get a fair hearing. That is why we need meetings of this nature up and down the country to be able to represent the true Muslim perspective on the issues that are facing us.

What is lacking, the speaker laments, is proper political organization and mobilization. Above all, in his committee stance, a man who believes in practical, tangible achievements, he lacks the kudos and personal mobilizing power to achieve these. He turns then to express his sense of frustration with the basic political inactivity of Muslims in Britain. He calls despairingly for more activism:

We have got to mobilize opinion so that the Muslims look at the Immigration Act in a different light. It threatens our religious life in this country. We need to mobilize, we need to march up and down Downing Street demanding that these rules be changed.

He then goes on to complain that in the field of education there is 'total discrimination and open discrimination'. While Church of England, Catholic and Jewish schools have all been granted state-aided status, Muslims are denied this right. 'Some phony reason is found by the Minister of Education to deny state-aided status to Muslim schools'. Finally, he turns to his audience:

We are a million Muslims and we are not capable of getting five thousand people to go to Downing Street to protest about this basic inhuman injustice! Mrs Thatcher was there, at the United Nations' Conference for children. There are a number of Muslim children, British born, British children, whose fathers are not able to live with them because of immigration rules, whose fathers are being deported, day and night, because of immigration rules. Why are we such dead people that we cannot stand up for our rights and fight? I don't say break windows, but fight, fight for rights by joining the political process in this country, by joining the demonstrations which are taking place, and by organizing demonstrations up and down the country to ask for your rights, because even when a child doesn't cry, the mother who doesn't give her milk fails. We are an Asian society and to preserve our rights, to preserve our identity, to preserve our integrity we need to fight, and fight hard. So be prepared from now on to lead that fight. Manchester has started, twelve years ago – the first procession in this country took place in Manchester twelve years ago to celebrate the birthday of the Prophet Muhammad [in fact, previous processions had been held in Birmingham]. And I say now that Manchester should give the lead on other issues. The celebration is not just to describe *eid milad un nabi*, but it is also about fighting for the rights of our people.

South Asian Islamic dissent and the fight for liberty

'Why are we such dead people?' We hear in these words the heart-felt call of the layman, the political activist, who evokes in his

populist rhetoric concrete images laced with calls for action. I turn
now, therefore, to these forgotten preachers of Islam.

The meeting in Manchester was organized by the local
vicegerent (*khalifa*) of a British-based, Sufi Qadri order, and the
majority of those attending were members or supporters of the
order. As a political-cum-religious movement these followers are
known collectively as *barelwi*. In Manchester, some of the *barelwi*
followers focused around the *maulvi* of the Central Mosque are
the most radical. In their processions on the Prophet's birthday
this group asserts the legitimacy of the movement in general, while
attesting also to the ascendancy of their particular Sufi regional
cult in the city.

Their radicalism could be explained in sectarian terms. During
the Rushdie affair they were enraged by the attack on the Prophet,
who is the subject of supreme adoration for *barelwi*. During the
Gulf crisis, support for Saddam Hussein stemmed from their
continuous opposition to the Wahabbi movement and its Saudi
rulers, regarded as the desecrators of saints' shrines throughout
Arabia, including that of the Prophet himself.

Nevertheless, the political radicalization of these faithful believ-
ers remains surprising because Sufi saints and their cults have been
regarded as politically dead for some time by Middle Eastern scholars. Their very existence as a contemporary political force is
denied. Hence, it has been argued for the Maghreb that while the
early fight against the colonial invasion was conducted by saintly
tribal leaders, once that battle was lost, the fight shifted to the
cities and was led by intellectual reformers, who engaged in a
class-cum-symbolic battle for cultural supremacy. The anthropologist Ernest Gellner constructs a series of dualistic oppositions –
between tribe and city, saint and Muslim scholar, syncretism and
reform, power and kinship, civilization and decadence, purity and
literacy, pluralism and monism, hierarchy and intercession and
egalitarianism – and believes the saints and their followers have
died out as a political force.

In South Asia, however, the reform movement met with powerful organized opposition in defence of Sufi saints and the cultic
practices surrounding their tombs. This 'counter-reformation'
unites Saints and scholars, *pirs* and *maulvis*, the charismatic elect
and the learned doctors, within a single organization. The scholars
have their own Islamic schools, usually known as *Dar-ul-Ulooms*,
their own networks, their mosques, their religious establishment
and their political party.

Reformer jurists and saintly jurists mirror each other's organizations and are locked in continuous religious controversy. The saints themselves rarely partake in these scholarly disputations. They use the *ulama* to provide religious services, deliver sermons, and organize religious institutions, while they themselves concentrate on the organization of their order, the recruitment of disciples, and the dispensing of divine blessing and healing to their devotees. Sometimes *pirs* are also learned men, while doctors sometimes become saints. On the whole, however, the saints disdain the *maulvis* while relying heavily upon their services.

Hence, in Pakistan the battle for religious ecstasy has never been lost, despite the institutionalization of religion. It is a battle conducted on both sides by Sunni, *Shari'a*-trained, learned doctors. As articulated intellectually by the *barelwis*, it is a battle between the heart and the mind, love and pedantic scholarship, ecstatic devotion and mere religious observance, mystical symbolism and lifeless literalism. It is, importantly, a modern, contemporary battle. In the course of this apparently purely religious dialogue, broader political issues are debated, and it is to these I wish to turn.

Since Islam has never had a centralized, established church, it has never had religious dissent in the specifically Christian sense. The real issue is when and why did a rhetoric of civil rights, democracy, equality and socialism expand beyond narrow, élitist modernist circles, to become part of a broad-based, popular South Asian religious ideology? In general it can be said that as the anti-British movement gathered pace in India, and as independence seemed imminent, virtually all the various religious groups, from landed charismatic saints to urban puritanical scholars, supported the cause of liberty against repressive, external domination. The problems of civil rights and liberation remained, however, the domain of the League and the modernists.

After Partition, 'liberty' became buried in conservative religious politics. Whereas the saints in rural areas engaged in quietist patronage power politics, the *ulama*, many of whom became once more employees of the state, also founded political parties which fought alongside and against each other for greater say and influence in the state apparatus.

Irrespective of political affiliation, however, it has always seemed impossible to conduct purely secular politics in Pakistan. Even the People's Party, which won the elections in West Pakistan on a socialist ticket, utilized an Islamic idiom and appeared to have relied increasingly upon saintly patronage to mobilize political support. Nationalism in Pakistan is inextricably intertwined with Islam, the *raison d'être* for the very existence of the state, and it has hitherto proved impossible to separate the two.

On one side, then, are the sober and determined puritanical reform scholars. Aligned against them are pacifist saints and fiery, populist scholars. The interest of the scholars on both sides remains, as before, to increase their political influence in the state or local community. They are not interested in civil liberties, economic equality or democratic rights. These have always been associated in Pakistani politics with secular or 'modernist' groups. But on either side is also a third element – lay preachers who are usually community leaders involved in mosque politics. In the present Islamic revival, it is they who articulate grassroots sentiments and help to explain the processes that have given rise to the current movement of Islamic radicalism.

Mosque, community and lay preachers

'Loyalty ultimately belongs to God, and I say there should be justice, there should be equality, there should be understanding, there should be humanity.' So proclaims one of the speakers at the meeting discussed here. The move from God to liberty and equality is not deductive; it is intuitive and emotional. We love God and the Prophet, hence we detest autocratic greedy leaders. Like lay Methodist preachers the men involved in mosque affairs speak for the ordinary man, not necessarily for the religious establishment of their particular brand of Islam. Indeed, it is my impression that they speak with the same political voice whatever Muslim religious movement or sect they happen to be affiliated to.

These lay preachers have introduced a radical change of rhetoric. Not Islamic authoritarianism but Islamic love, equality and individual liberties. Yet the underlying tension between love and authoritarianism within the movement itself is also evident (as it was in Methodism). *Barelwis* do not need to be rich, learned, educated or prominent. All they need in order to qualify as good Muslims is to love the Prophet of Islam and his *awliya* (his chosen 'friends', i.e. Sufi saints). The movement is an essentially egalitarian one. At the same time its leaders, Sufi shaikhs, are highly authoritarian. Yet, paradoxically, it is precisely because they are spiritually superior, by birth and ascetic practice, to temporal, powerful, wealthy monarchs and rulers, that their disciples feel able to challenge the legitimacy of those leaders, and to make demands for equal political and economic rights.

Hence, rather than a neat, logical, dualistic alternation model, positing a series of corresponding opposites, saints and scholars, and so forth, what exists empirically, on the ground as it were, is a complex set of three independent interacting social categories – saints, scholars and laymen – allied together within a single movement. Between them they negotiate the rhetorical narratives of contemporary religious dissent. The oscillation is an internal one – between quietism or conservatism and radical populism – and it is related, above all, to the interpretations of political events and constellations as these are perceived to impinge on the actors, either as direct participants, or as members of broader Muslim communities, national and transnational.

The speeches at the town hall in Manchester combined theology, especially the adoration of the Prophet and his exemplary life, with a stress on the pride of bearing an Islamic identity and the uniqueness of being Muslim. At the same time the radical challenge to the established order was unmistakable. The attack was three-pronged: against the injustice of international law and global decision-making, both of which ignored Muslim national interests; against the corrupt illegitimate regimes of the Gulf states, denying the economic rights of 'ordinary Muslims'; and against British legal discrimination which denied local Muslims their basic rights as citizens. If the latter referred to immediate local interests, speakers clearly felt that their specific complaints could only be addressed in broader, more global and general terms. Hence the unmitigated radicalism of the participants.

There are other parallels to be drawn with the late eighteenth and early nineteenth century 'labour sects' in Britain, which the cultural historians E.P. Thompson and Eric Hobsbawm have written about. The mosque, like the chapel, is the centre of communal affairs, drawing labour migrants into communal activities. It is the base for teaching collective discipline, organization and internal fund raising, the springboard for regional and national political alliances, a training ground in polemics and adversary politics.

The link between saints and doctors among *barelwis* means that the movement is a powerful urban, as well as rural, organization. Indeed, it creates organic links between town and village, and its lodges and mosques provide welcoming havens and communal centres for migrant travellers.

Mosques – in the plural, for they have proliferated in British cities – are supported not only by Pakistani factory workers but by small shopkeepers, market traders, small manufacturers, artisans, professionals and a few bigger businessmen. These are all men with a sense of individual pride, a measure of personal autonomy, who hold strong ideas about the rights due to them as citizens and productive workers. They are not people to be pushed around. Yet they lack real political power and influence in Britain and this powerlessness has been underlined in recent years by the Rushdie affair, the general increase in racial harassment, and the Gulf crisis.

Parallels may be drawn with the Iranian revolution in which the urban *bazaaris* played, it is argued, an important role. There too, analysts have shown, Shi'a Islam shifted from a quiescent symbolic interpretation of martyrdom as suffering, to an activist view of martyrdom as personal sacrifice for the sake of a cause. The radicalization of urban Iranians arose in response to a sense of direct attack by the state on the clergy and the urban lower-middle-and working-classes who had been relatively autonomous and mobile socially.

Mosques are central foci of communal activity for local British Muslim communities. They bring together Muslim religious experts and local community activists, and the dialogue between these two groups, enacted publicly during ceremonials or religious meetings, has generated greater political awareness, even in groups normally opportunistic and quiescent, such as those of *barelwi* followers. Until recently, however, most mosques in Britain, and most religious leaders, remained politically introverted, engaged mainly in internecine religious conflicts and factional rivalries. The publication of *The Satanic Verses* marked a watershed in this state of affairs: it revealed the need for broader organizational frameworks, as well as setting new agendas for common action, required in order to challenge the state and its current laws. The Gulf crisis sharpened this need for political protest and added further complexity to the emergent political philosophy articulated from mosque pulpits and communal podiums.

Under these circumstances it is perhaps not surprising that British Pakistanis paid little heed to the price they might pay for their dissenting support for Saddam Hussein. Although their statements were only semi-official, and they often retracted the most radical statements when questioned publicly by the media, it seems quite clear that they wanted the wider society to be aware of their disaffection. Theirs was a confrontational posture, as yet not fully worked out, more protest than actual action. The swings between temporary utopian hopes for Islamic dominance, and a sense of communal failure and total powerlessness, are more evident in British Muslims' attitudes than any determination to engage in sustained practical political action. During these swings, what is continuously elaborated is a politically constituted religious rhetoric, a rhetoric of dissent, which above all narrates the particular place of British Pakistani immigrants, as 'ordinary Muslims' within Britain, and the broader, international Muslim world.

8

NATION, NATION-STATE AND POLICY TOWARDS ETHNIC MINORITIES

FRIEDRICH HECKMANN

My concern here is not directly with Muslim populations in Europe, but with major social and political interrelations between the nation-state and immigrant populations as new ethnic minorities. Since Muslim populations figure largely in these minorities, the relation of nation-state to ethnic minorities is a central aspect of their existence in European societies. With particular reference then to Germany. What are the problems that Muslim miniorities – and other immigrant groups – face as a result of majority policies?

Ethnicity

In its most general meaning 'ethnicity' stands for the social fact that groups share elements of culture, past and/or present experiences; they hold a belief in a common descent, share a concept of collective identity and definitions of belonging and on that basis develop a sense of solidarity. Belief in a common descent being the most important defining element, ethnic relations could be called quasi-genealogical relations (Heckmann, 1992, pp. 41–79).

Depending on historical context and type of group formation, ethnic collectivities have been specified as tribe, race, people, nation, ethnic group and ethnic minority.

I work on the assumption that ethnicity and ethnic collectivities are universal phenomena and concepts, with historically varying, quite differing meanings and social relevance. In more concrete

terms, although ethnicity is an increasingly important phenomenon in the modern world, nevertheless it is not always relevant
when members of ethnic groups interact with one another or with
members of other ethnic groups. 'It is not always the most appropriate principle around which social activity or identity may be
organized' (Wallman, 1972). If ethnicity takes on importance, its
effects can be quite different. It can be a resource which will, for
some purposes and in some situations, be mobilized to the advan-
tage of a social, cultural or racial group of people, but it will have
no meaning or value at all in other situations, and could, in yet
other situations, be regarded as a liability to be escaped or denied
as far as possible (ibid.).

If these hypotheses refer to a differing situational relevance of
ethnicity one has to add that the relevance of ethnicity varies with
large scale macrosocietal and historical forms of social organization: the importance of shared ethnicity as a principle of social
organization differs with the general type of society (Francis,
1965).

The modern nation-state makes ethnicity a central part of its
social and political organization. How did this come about? Ancient
and mediaeval empires did not attribute major relevance to ethnicity as a principle of socio-political organization. There were no
nations in our sense of the term. There were ethnic groups but no
peoples or large ethnic collectivities, such as French, Germans or
Russians. In contrast to the romantic concept of *Volk* as an *Urvolk*
(i.e. a naturally grown cultural community), a modern sociological
concept emphasizes that *Volk* is a product of historical process.
Through migration, change of authority and borders, by war and
peace, occupation and conquest, everywhere populations of very
different origins and characteristics have been moved, mixed or
made to coexist. The composition of populations may be quite
correctly called the result of a random process (Kimminich, 1985,
pp. 31–2).

However, diversity has not remained as it once existed. Through
processes of social communication and homogenization, which
started with the development of territorial states, economic, political and cultural integration has taken place: the formation of new
languages, patterns of acculturation and assimilation have led to
ethnic homogenization and created populations who actually came
to share certain common cultural and historical characteristics.

Ethnic nationalism added to this a belief, an ideology, that
certain populations had a common origin and history which made

them into a *Volk*. A total revision of history was undertaken to support this view. Dead languages were revived, 'traditions invented, quite fictitious pristine purities restored' (Gellner, 1983, p. 56).

Ethnic nationalism

Ethnic nationalism appeared in Germany in the eighteenth century, but became a political ideology and social movement during the nineteenth century. It has gained considerable new momentum in contemporary Eastern Europe. As a political ideology, ethnic nationalism seeks to establish ethnicity as the basis of legitimation for state organization: ethnic and state-political borders should be identical.

This ethnically based nation-state, according to its internal logic, also creates ethnic minorities. The attempt to build ethnically homogeneous political states – due to historically given settlement patterns – creates ethnic minorities. Ethnic minorities are constituted, when ethnic majorities form as nations following the concept of ethnic homogeneity. Ethnic heterogeneity, which was and still is a reality in most states, is looked upon by the ethnic nation-state as a problem to be solved or controlled so ethnic antagonism between majority and minority develops. The working of this logic with its destructive results can be clearly seen at the time of writing all over South Eastern and Eastern Europe.

In Germany, Herder's concept of *Volk* had been part of enlightened and humanitarian thinking. *'Alles Ethnische ist ... Ausdruck des Humanen: die Humanität erscheint nur durch das Medium der Nationalität'* (Schieder, 1978, p. 122). German idealist philosophers and nationalists, such as Fichte and Arndt, however, closely connected ideas of ethnicity with state organization and state boundaries, and with ethnic antagonism toward ethnic minorities. Members of a single ethnic collectivity, and no one else, should form a unified political structure. To quote Paul de Lagard:[1]

Es ist zweifellos nicht statthaft, daß in irgendeiner Nation eine andere Nation bestehe; es ist zweifellos geboten, diejenigen, welche ... jene Dekomposition befördert haben, zu beseitigen: es ist das Recht jedes Volkes, selbst Herr auf seinem Gebiet zu sein, für sich zu leben, nicht für Fremde (quoted in Lenk, 1971).

In Fichte's and Arndt's writings there is also an aggressive attitude toward ethnic minorities, in particular Slavs and Jews.

A people aspiring for or having achieved 'their' state organization were called a nation and 'their' state a nation-state. The ethnic nation-state was claimed to be a 'natural' order (Schieder, 1978). Ethnicity had played no major role in the mediaeval political system: the territorial state was ideologically integrated by loyalty to the prince. In the (ethnic) nation-state, however, ethnicity became the major principle of legitimacy upon which state organization was based.

The political implications of national ideology were:

1. To form nation states through unification movements, when members of a large ethnic body were living in different states (as in Italy or Germany).
2. To try to assimilate or segregate those parts of a state's population that were of different ethnic origin and characteristics.

Political nationalism

Ethnic nationalism and the nation-state based on ethnicity should be differentiated from a political concept of nation and nation-state. Political nations define their community as consisting of common values, beliefs, traditions and institutions, not in terms of common ethnicity. The political, non-ethnic nation concept can be further subdivided into (a) a so-called demotic-unitarian nation; and (b) an ethnically plural nation.

The demotic-unitarian nation

The concept of demotic-unitarian nation can be illustrated by the case of France. Nation, before, during and after the French Revolution, is a political term. In the French Revolution nation stands for the claim to legitimate power by the *tiers état*. In the well-known words of Abbé Sieyès:

Le tiers état inclut tous ceux qui appartiennent à la nation: ceux qui n'appartiennent pas au tiers état n'appartiennent pas à la nation. Une nation est une union d'individus gouvernés par une seule loi et représentés par une même assemblée respectueuse de cette loi.

Thus, it is correct to say that the basic concept of the French Revolution was not that of Frenchman, but of *citoyen*. People, *Volk* in the political nation concept, means something very different from the ethnic concept. It denotes the tradition, founded by the Enlightenment and the French Revolution, to base political authority on the sovereignty of the people. People, in this sense, is a non-ethnic political and legal concept, originally formulated in opposition to the teaching of the sovereignty of the prince; it stands for a political community which is at the same time the source of political authority. Much confusion would be avoided if a clear differentiation between the ethnic and the political meaning of *Volk*, between ethnos and demos, was made (Francis, 1965; Lepsius, 1986).

The ethnically plural nation

The ethnically plural nation concept can be briefly illustrated by the Swiss case. The political nation concept reveals itself in the myth of William Tell:

When the influence of nationalism made itself felt, the Swiss did not attempt to found their unity on the myth of a common descent or language, but on common political traditions and institutions. They turned for inspiration to their past struggles for constitutional liberty – back to the thirteenth century. They revived the memory and glorified the interpretation of those foundations: William Tell became a national hero. (Francis, 1965).

The common institutions in Switzerland are based on sophisticated applications of principles of federalism, of interest, mediation and compromise (*Vernehmlassungsverfahren*). The political system has a high degree of legitimacy.

Nation concepts and policy toward ethnic minorities

In regard to these three concepts of nation and nation-state – ethnic nation, demotic-unitarian and plural nation – can a relation be established between the type of nation and policy towards ethnic minorities?

Ethnic nation-state and policy towards ethnic minorities

To the ethnic nation and the ethnic nation-state, ethnic heterogeneity, by its very principles, is a problem to be rid of or, at least, to control. Ethnic nationalism is not only a general pattern of political legitimation, but a concept that determines concrete policy toward ethnic minorities. This can be briefly demonstrated in three areas of policy with regard to Germany: acculturation or assimilation; citizenship and naturalization; political participation.

In the first instance, for the ethnic nation-state, ethnic minorities on its territory are a threat to its claim to ethnic homogeneity; in its homogenization drive the state tries to assimilate ethnic minorities. Overwhelming evidence from many countries supports this hypothesis. In Germany, for instance, even before the Nazi period, the state conducted a severe Germanization policy towards its Polish and Danish minorities.

As regards citizenship and naturalization, since the nation defines itself in terms of common descent and history, ethnic and citizen are closely related and tied to one another, both as concepts and in respect of legal status. In the case of Germany, ethnic Germans from Eastern Europe who migrate to the Federal Republic – *Aussiedler* – are regarded and treated as citizens. On the other hand, and quite logically, naturalization is a difficult process and rather an exception with the ethnic nation-state. Children of immigrants, born in Germany and living there remain 'foreigners'. '*On entre difficilement dans un groupe fondé sur les liens de nature*' (Schnapper...). The empirical validity of this argument can be easily demonstrated by looking at German naturalization statistics. German law recognizes two types of naturalization:

1. *Anspruchseinbürgerungen*, a type reserved for foreign persons married to Germans;
2. So-called *Ermessenseinbürgerungen* for all other persons.

The figures for this second type are the more valid indicator for naturalization policy. In 1975, for instance, there were about 10,000 cases of *Ermessenseinbürgerungen*; in 1979 about 15,000; and in 1984 about 14,000. With a non-German population of around 4.4 million in 1984, the naturalization rate for that year was 0.003 per cent (Huber, 1987). This trend continues.

Because of the close link between ethnic and citizen status and belonging, the principle '*Alle Staatsgewalt geht vom Volke aus*' tends to be interpreted in an ethnically restrictive way and to exclude, as the highest federal court has recently confirmed, residents without citizenship from even the lower levels of political participation. This argument does not overlook the fact that immigrants themselves have to rethink their attitudes about citizenship, the acquisition of which is supposedly easier under the new *Ausländergesetz*. A relevant breakthrough in naturalization would imply a weakening of the ethnic nation concept. We have to wait and see what comes out this recent development.

Demotic-unitarian nation and ethnic minorities

Political nationalism would be misunderstood if it were interpreted as representing a positive attitude toward 'multiculturalism'. As Francis states:

> The homogenization of the state population, which the absolute state had initiated by accident rather than by deliberate design, became a task of the utmost urgency for the nation state. For the state was now viewed as the politically organized nation ... the legitimacy and proper functioning of democratic government required that the citizens should form a viable societal unit having a corporate will. It was therefore the right and duty of the nation-state to remove all obstacles to this unity of purpose: to eradicate – if need be by brute police force – all the traditional identities and particularistic solidarities, including those based on shared ethnicity, which divided the state population (Francis, 1965).

Among other facts, the language policy of the French Revolution could be mentioned to support this argument. *'Terreur' linguistique* is the key word here. The foregoing argument in this that the demotic nation state has both a homogenization and assimilation tendency toward ethnic heterogeneity. There are, however, relevant differences that are not to be overlooked. Since the demotic nation concept is not based on ethnicity, it is more open towards immigrants:

> *par son principe même de légitimité, l'appartenance à la nation française est ouverte (au moins dans l'idéal) à tous ceux qui sont prêts à*

adopter ses valeurs. L'identité nationale n'est pas un fait biologique, mais culturelle: on est Français par la pratique d'une langue, par l'intériorisation d'une culture, par la volonté de participer à la vie économique et politique (Schnapper). In terms of concrete policy, this openness is evident in the case of naturalization of immigrants and the automatic or semi-automatic forms of naturalization for children of immigrants. When naturalization is easy, exclusion of non-citizens from political participation is, of course, much less of a problem.

Plural nation-state and policy toward ethnic minorities

Regarding the third type of nation-state, the ethnically plural organization, one could say that by its very principles, this nation-state shows tolerance towards ethnic heterogeneity; it is even based on ethnic heterogeneity, on a political treaty between different ethnic groups. However, an important difference exists between those who legally belong to the nation and those who do not. For those who belong, a sophisticated system of autonomy and protection of cultural rights exists, when in a minority situation. Switzerland may serve as an illustration of this.

In principle, the political, ethnically plural nation-state may show tolerance towards immigrant minorities as well, since it is not based on ethnic homogeneity. The discrimination and ethnic aversion we also find here, however, could be explained as stemming from society, not from principles of state legitimacy and organization.

A word of caution

However, the foregoing arguments in regard to principles of minority policy in different types of nation-state are not the whole picture. They represent 'ideally typical' modes of legitimation of nation, nation-state and nation-state policy. Undoubtedly they have a real influence, but in reality they could not be found in the pure form as depicted here; and they are only part of a reality which in effect includes many other forces both supporting or counteracting its influence. To give a single, but important, example, the excluding or assimilating forces of ethnic nationalism today come up against modern democratic ideas, principles of equal rights and of human rights, which do not permit ethnic discrimination, segregation or cultural repression. The consequences of these conflicts have to be analysed in concrete instances. My aim has been to show some basic structures and strains that underlie situations of 'multiculturalism' in the modern world.

The 'ideally typical' argument is also revealed in what has been said about Germany and France as representing the ethnic nation-state type, on the one hand, and the political nation type, on the other. The 'real' France also has characteristics of an ethnic nation (one speaks of '*Français de souche*' for instance), just as the 'real' Germany has traits of a political nation (the recent easing of natu-ralization via the new *Ausländergesetz*). But inter-ethnic relations within modern states are not only an internal problem of states and societies. They exist within the structure of international relations.

Foreign policy, nation-state and ethnic minorities

Four areas and types of policy are differentiated: irredentism, 'support', the minority as an instrument in the policy of a foreign state and minority policy as a legitimation problem of a state.

Irrenditism

Irredentism is a political movement within a nation-state and an ethnically 'belonging' minority in a different state; its goal is to integrate the minority and its territory into the ethnic nation state. Irredentism is a dangerous movement that threatens peace, since it wants to change existing borders and treaties between states.

Irredentism has to be differentiated from the policy of a state to support – culturally, economically and politically – a 'belonging' ethnic minority in another state. There exists a treaty between Germany and Denmark, for instance, defining support relations both for the German minority in Denmark and the Danish minority in Germany on a reciprocal basis in each case, political rights in the form of political representation and cultural and educational autonomy are guaranteed.

The minority as an instrument of foreign policy

The support relation is again different from a policy in which an ethnically 'belonging' minority is the instrument of foreign policy of a nation-state. In extreme cases of this type the minority becomes the spearhead of an aggressive and expansionist foreign policy; German minorities in Eastern Europe during the Nazi period could be taken as an example. The fear of Islamic minorities in Europe becoming the spearhead of missionary and aggressive Islamic states is of the same type. The instrumental relation between nation-state and minority is a dangerous and peace-threatening pattern of foreign policy. A variation of this instrumental type is found in the relation between 'mother country' and emigrant minorities in migration processes. For political and economic reasons, the 'mother' nation tries to retain control over the part of its population that has 'settled' in the country of immigration.

Minority policy as a legitimation of foreign policies

The fourth type of relation to be identified is that between a nation-state and an ethnically foreign minority within its territory. The way in which a nation-state treats ethnic minorities within its territory affects its credibility and prestige in an international context; minority policy in this context is part of the legitimation process of foreign policy in a particular state. Thus, for example, the treatment of ethnic minorities in Germany is strongly related to the legitimation of Germany's foreign policy, and serves as a criterion of the degree to which Germans have 'really changed' in relation to the Nazi period.

Policy options for organizing majority-minority relations

The first pattern has been called *'national-kulturelle Autonomie'* by its Austrian inventor, Otto Bauer. It is a system of personal autonomy, in which the granting of certain rights and protection is given on the basis of ethnic belonging (i.e. not on a territorial base). The handling of this personal autonomy necessitates the existence of some kind of list (*cataster*), which holds the names of persons who are entitled to enjoy certain rights. Personal autonomy seems an attractive model, since it promises to fit the complex reality of ethnically mixed populations in a territory. *'Sie durchbricht das herkömmliche Schema des Denkens über Staat und*

Volksgruppe und läßt sozusagen die Kollektivrechte vom Individuum tragen' (Kimminich, 1985).

However, territorial autonomy is preferred by most authors on this subject, the exercise of rights including certain forms of law-making, here being tied to living in a territory.

Federalism is also a principle of political organization that rests on a territorial base. The 'centre' and the federal units have divided powers and rights, which in the case of multi-ethnic states allows for the organization of ethnic rights and protection as part of the general decentralizing of control. A confederacy would be a variation of the principles of federalism.

The protection of ethnic minorities may be further organized through international law (i.e. minority protection treaties). After World War I a large system of such treaties was created in Europe. In most cases, however, minority protection treaties were regarded by the nation-states as limitations to their sovereignty and did not prove to be an effective instrument of peacekeeping.

The foregoing patterns all have to do with collective rights. They are distinct from regulations that help members of a minority as individuals to exercise common rights. The institution of Ombudsman is an attempt to realize this. A rigorous policy of ensuring the exercise of constitutional rights 'for everyone' would also be advantageous to minorities. Probably there is no better 'minority policy' than a 'socially responsible' democratic and liberal state (*'freiheitlicher und sozialer Rechtsstaat'*), with a well-functioning economy and control over the immigration process. Anti-discrimination laws and/or affirmative action might be charac-teristics of such a state as well.

Relating some of these policy patterns to the different types of legitimation of nation and nation-state that we discussed above, one might say that personal and territorial autonomy is realized most easily in the plural nation-state. Both the ethnic and the demotic nation-state face problems in accepting territorial or personal autonomy. Least resistance in any type of nation-state can be expected from patterns of minority policy that are based on individual rights: unlike group rights for minorities, individual rights do not seem to limit the concept of sovereignty of the nation state.

Thus far, the arguments presented have been primarily of a general nature. In conclusion, a few – more specific – remarks are needed about the most urgent political problems facing immigrant minorities (including Muslim minorities) in Germany.

Nation state and immigrant minorities in Germany

During the 1970s the key word in the political discussion about *Gastarbeiter* was that of 'integration'. *'multikulturelle Gesellschaft'* (multicultural society) has become the centre of controversial political debate in the late 1980s and early 1990s. Understood by some people as a terrifying idea and by others as a descriptive category, still others praise it as a positive normative concept.

All three interpretations of multicultural society, however, are somewhat biased. There is neither a threat to German 'national identity', nor does the change in the ethnic composition of the population mean the dissolution of a previously homogeneous structure into ethnically heterogeneous segments. Nor is it likely that traditional national ideas will turn overnight into attitudes of cultural pluralism and internationalism. The debate, however, is evidence of an important change in Germany society. The foreign migrants who, supposedly, would have left after a few years' work, have 'settled', have become part of the population: the ethnic composition of the population has changed.

This change could be more adequately described by avoiding 'multicultural society' as a category and by turning to four major problem areas to describe the situation of immigrants in German society: *Ausländerstatus* (foreigner's status); political participation of non-citizens; level of new immigration; and future of the nation-state.

The main problem of the new immigrant minorities may be formulated as 'being present but not belonging'. Despite membership in different institutions, from the economy to the obligation to pay taxes, non-citizenship status and other forms of exclusion or closure constitute a specific status of non-belonging, *Ausländerstatus*. To be a foreigner is not something merely technical in a legal sense, it affects the whole of life. The *Ausländerstatus* is defined legally by the *Ausländergesetz*, which might be more adequately termed a law to control foreigners. *(Ausländerkontrollgesetz)*. Procedures and conflicts regarding migrants revolve around questions of allowance or refusal to stay, around incentives for return migration, around rights of family reunion *and* of being granted or refused certain welfare allowances – not around the 'classical' question of minority status which I discussed above.

Because naturalization is infrequent and dual citizenship is not allowed, it is difficult to relinquish foreigner's status. Particularly for the three million and more immigrants from non-EC countries, '*Ausländerstatus*' means being the object of discrimination and prejudice. To change the social perception of '*Ausländerstatus*' is difficult too. Non-citizens cannot organize civil rights campaigns. Classical solutions of ethnic minority problems, such as territorial or personal autonomy and minority protection treaties, presuppose citizenship as well.

Another central aspect of immigrant status in Germany is the exclusion from political participation and political rights. This means excluding a relevant section of the industrial working class from voting rights, a situation reminiscent of the nineteenth century. For a country with a democratic constitution and democratic ideals such exclusion from political participation creates serious problems of legitimation. Even if, as a consequence of the Maastricht EC decisions, immigrants from EC countries receive communal voting rights, for the large majority of the immigrant population (and for German society) the problem will persist.

A third problem that is often seen as a major theme in discussions about 'multicultural society' is the level of further immigration. Hundreds of thousands of immigrants each year over the last decade have contributed to the creation of resource shortages in the social structure; a continuation of large-scale immigration would further aggravate these shortages, particularly in housing, employment, education and public services. A mobilization of ethnic prejudice could well occur if immigration continues at the same level.

Given that Germany cannot solve the problems of Eastern Europe on its own territory, there has to be regulation and restriction of future immigration. Public discussion about an immigration law has begun and is linked to the emotional and sometimes demagogic debate about the right of asylum, which has in part become a substitute for labour immigration.

Finally, a fourth problem area that is touched upon in discussions of multiculturalism is the future of the nation-state or, to be more precise, of the ethnic nation-state. To move from an ethnic nation concept in the direction of a more political nation concept, on the basis of a political and legal understanding of *Volk*, would contribute to changing the traditional ethnic idea of citizenship and naturalization in Germany. The ethnic nation concept, though prominent again in Eastern and South-Eastern Europe is less significant in Western Europe because of increasing political, economic and military internationalization. A demotic, open concept of nation should include policies of acculturation and assimilation, as well as affording opportunities for minority peoples, but would not condone ethnic activities leading to ethnic self-isolation. Self-isolation and self-sufficiency among ethnic minorities in communities or colonies of their own – particularly strong among Muslim immigrants – prevents such people playing a full part in the competition for highly valued positions in society. Many of those who support the idea of a multicultural society emotionally tend to overlook this important point. 'Progressive' multiculturalism and ethnic self-assertion both in the dominant majority and the minorities, though they are in vocal opposition in public, in fact, together contribute to segmenting immigrant minorities along the lines of their ethnicity.

Note

1. Paul de Lagarde, pseudonym of Paul Anton Botticher (1827–1891), philosopher and orientalist, whose extreme nationalism became a source of Nazi ideology.

9

CHANGES IN TURKISH MIGRANT FAMILIES IN GERMANY

BERNHARD NAUCK

Social scientists have invariably made far-reaching assumptions on changes in family structure because of international migration. No dimension of family structure has been exempted from the guess that it might be influenced drastically by migration: considerations about the social organization of life courses and family life cycles, about mate selection, generative behaviour, employment (of mothers) have played an important role, just as have considerations about changes in inter- and intragenerational relationships and in the social participation, kinship relations and social networks of the family members. This has to be said by way of introduction because – as far as Germany is concerned – no attempts have been made so far to test these far-reaching assumptions on social changes in migrant families empirically, for example by longitudinal studies. Up to now, in fact, no single longitudinal study on changes in migrant families has been made. This is the more astonishing as none of the several textbooks on the social consequences of migration or on the education of migrant minorities fails to include a chapter on the Turkish family (i.e. 'traditional', 'patriarchal', 'Islamic', 'rural', 'uneducated' which in contrast to the German family is the most 'exotic' of all migrant minorities (or at least the one at the greatest social distance), so depicting the disruptive changes and conflicts in such migrant families in vivid colours. It has to be stressed that most of these assertions result from (very few) cross-sectional surveys of (mostly not very systematically chosen) migrants – if their 'empirical basis' is not derived from interpretations of the Koran or of Islamic legislation. These 'results' have been strongly generalized afterwards and have acquired their own folklore by repeated citations, but they were seldom compared systematically to the (easily available) empirical family research in Turkey. The main aim of what follows is therefore to summarize the empirical findings on changes in the structure of Turkish migrant families.

Social change to migrant families can be studied at three different levels of analysis: Changes in social structure; intergenerational changes and intragenerational changes.

Changes in social structure

Time series can be established on the basis of population statistics, which show periodic changes in the quantitative distribution of family structures and the demographic composition of the migrant population.

Intergenerational changes

Comparisons between different cohorts of migrant families relating to the date of migration can show long-term changes of family structure in migrant minorities, and the distinction between 'first generation' migrant families (migrants born and socialized in their country of origin and/or married 'under the contract conditions' of their homeland) and members of the 'second generation' (those born and/or married in the 'host' country (i.e. Germany), or 'third generation' (who do not as yet exist in Germany).

Intragenerational changes

Comparisons of the family structure at different points during migration experience can show the interrelationship of endogenous factors in the family life cycle and exogenous factors of migration and assimilation and related factors such as a changed ecological context, opportunity structures or social networks. These age-dependent changes in migrant families can be analysed with respect to three major dimensions: intragenerational relationships (between spouses), intergenerational relationships (between parents and children) and kinship relationships.

In any case, most of the research on migrant families in Germany refers to the Turkish minority. It is not only the largest minority in Germany, but of major theoretical and methodological importance as well. As comparative analyses have shown, the assimilation processes of members of this minority do not differ systematically from those of other minorities (Hill, 1984).

The analysis that follows is centred on inter- and intragenerational changes in Turkish migrant families in Germany. Additional analyses on demographic and sociostructural changes in migrant families have been made elsewhere (Nauck 1988, 1992).

Intergenerational changes in Turkish migrant families

Until now, empirical answers to the question of direction and intensity of intergenerational changes in migrant families in Germany have only been possible in a very rudimentary form. This is not due to any lack of scientific interest in the question. On the contrary, intergenerational changes have always played a very prominent role in explaining assimilation processes since the conceptualization of the 'race relations cycles' in the 1930s (Essor, 1980; Treibre, 1990). They have often been adopted to explain behavioural changes in migrant minorities in Germany, presupposing that the changed cultural conditions at the time of primary socialization – and its life-long importance for the internalization of values – results in an 'inevitable' acculturation and evident value differences and social conflicts between the first and second generation of immigrants (Schrader et al., 1979). But for historical reasons, families of the second generation of immigrants have until now been few, so that the scope of investigation has been limited to socialization processes, youth conflicts and changes in marriage attitudes, whereas comparative research on family structures must wait until the future. In a representative 1984 sample of Turkish families with at least one child between 6 and 16 years, no single parent was found who had lived in Germany since birth. In a representative 1985 survey of foreigners over 15 years (König et al., 1986) only 2.6 per cent were born in Germany (1.0 per cent of Turks and 7.1 per cent of Italians), but they were almost all younger than 25 and unmarried, so that this sample comprised fewer than 0.5 per cent married foreigners of the second generation and conclusions on intergenerational changes are impossible.

However, these results do allow conclusions on changes in attitudes towards marriage. In a replication survey of 1980 and 1985 a remarkable decrease in marriage plans is to be observed for non-married work migrants.

Whereas in 1980 54.7 per cent of non-married work migrants in Germany had marriage in mind, in 1985 this proportion fell to 35.4 per cent. The decrease is especially marked for young work migrants and for Turks (as compared with Italians) and comprises both sexes. In 1980 58.0 per cent of unmarried male Turkish work migrants and 50.2 per cent of females planned to marry, but in 1985 this proportion had dropped to 22.1 per cent and 17.6 per cent respectively. With Italian migrants the decrease was significantly lower (62.0 per cent to 51.5 per cent for males and 58.0 per cent to 47.8 per cent for females). Over the same period a positive attitude towards marriage with a German partner increased (from 42.6 per cent to 48.6 per cent). But while for Italians, as an earlier immigrant nationality, this positive attitude remained stable at a fairly high level (55.5 per cent) for the Turks the rise was more striking (from 27.8 per cent to 35.8 per cent). Again a more positive attitude was shown on the part of the Turkish men (49.1 per cent) than on the part of Turkish women (13.8 per cent) and a more equal distribution of attitudes in both sexes in the Italian migrant minority (58.3 per cent against 50.6 per cent). These results on attitudes in population surveys are thus consistent with the data reported before on demographic social changes.

It is of theoretical importance that the positive attitudes towards bi-national marriages is not higher in the second generation foreigners born in Germany than in the first generation of work migrants. On the contrary, these positive attitudes are strongest in the group of first generation migrants whose stay has been longer. Positive attitudes towards intermarriage do not increase with the stay in the 'host' society (as a result of assimilation process) but with age (as a result of decreasing alternatives on the marriage market). While 45 per cent of unmarried foreigners under 30 are willing to marry a German, this proportion increases to 60 per cent for the older foreigners. These phenomena draw attention to the fact that analysis of inter- and intragenerational changes must distinguish three difference processes: changes in opportunity structure, migration and assimilation experience, and family life cycle.

Historic changes in the opportunity structure

Besides changes in political and economic conditions for foreigners in the host country, changes in the size of the foreign population have especially to be mentioned here. Unlike later migrants, the pioneer migrants found no ethnic minority in place at the time of their arrival and were thus obliged to assimilate on their own. Results from retrospective interviews show that the consumption of German TV programmes is reduced since there is now a better supply of Turkish video films and even original Turkish TV programmes, which can be received directly via satellite. More than half the Turkish families now have kinship relations within Germany.

Changes in migration- and assimilation-experience

Historic changes in context opportunities have to be separated from changes in the individual course of migration and assimilation. The timing of migration in relation to age clearly leads to different alternatives with respect to assimilation and segregation. Of course, such assimilation experience is time- and energy-consuming so that duration of stay is a necessary, if not a sufficient, condition for assimilative changes in migrant families.

Changes in the family life cycle

Migrant families undergo indigenous family dynamics as well as any other family. In particular, alternatives for assimilation change in view of previous personal and family decisions such as marrying early or late, leaving spouse and/or children behind, or having many or few children.

The influence of these three processes on changes in migrant families has not yet been fully studied, and empirical analyses of interactions between these processes are only now beginning. Intergenerational changes of interaction structures in migrant families can be studied so far on the basis of comparison between families, started before or after migration. Results from Turkish migrant families show that those families that were 'contracted' under the conditions of the 'host' society differ considerably from those what existed already at the time of migration.

There is a consistent pattern in the change of generative behaviour. The higher the cognitive assimilation of Turkish migrant woman (language acquisition), the higher the structural assimilation (household income, living comfort) and the more modernized the family lifestyle (refusal of normative sex-role orientation and economic-utilitarian VOC; preference for psychological VOC), the earlier the generative cycle is finished and the lower is the completed fertility rate.

Turkish migrant families 'contracted' under the conditions of the 'host' society show remarkably different generative behaviour to families that already existed at the time of migration. The probability for a Turkish woman of having 4 children is for those who migrated before marriage or the birth of their first child only 15 per cent or 18 per cent respectively, whereas it is 50 per cent of all Turkish migrant families. High numbers of children in migrant families, a subject which dominated public debate for a long time, are due to the fact that the wives remained for a long time in Turkey and were 'imported' by family reunion. Thus, migration leads to a drastic restructuring of their lives: 50 per cent of women, who stayed on in their homeland and with less than obligatory schooling are married at the age of 17.5 and finish their generative cycle at the age of 38.4 with the birth of a fifth child; the same percentage of the women, who migrated early and with at least obligatory schooling, are not married before 20.4 and finish their generative cycle at the age of 39.3 with the birth of a third child only.

Differences in attitude

Differences in attitude between families contracted in Turkey and those contracted in Germany are visible with respect to normative sex-role orientations, (e.g. the tendency to relate specific role contents and expectations to sex, measured by a short form of the sex-role orientation (SRO) scale (Brogan and Kutner, 1976). Turkish fathers and mothers who married in Germany have a significantly lower normative sex-role orientation than those who were married already when they migrated. No differences are visible with respect to self-perceived educational attitudes. Turkish parents of the 'second generation' are only slightly less overprotective, less authoritarian and more permissive than parents from the 'first generation' of migrants. A thorough analysis of the separate parent-child relationships shows that only the father-daughter dyad has undergone revision. Fathers of the 'second generation' are far more self-confident and less critical in their behaviour towards their daughter, less authoritarian and more permissive than fathers of the first generation.

Behaviour differences

There are considerable differences between the behaviour of first and second generation Turkish migrant families. Turkish families begun in Germany show a very strong tendency towards 'rationalization' of early child-care practices. Compared to families begun in Turkey the duration of breastfeeding is reduced from 10.2 months to 3.3 months, and the proportion of families which prefer fixed time schedules for feeding in early childhood increases from 57 per cent to 85 per cent. Differences are also obvious in familial socialization. The institutional stimulation of the child outside school (e.g. by recourse to public libraries, membership of sports clubs, participation in leisure groups, private lessons) is significantly higher in second generation families, and girls especially profit from this development, so that – contrary to first generation Turkish migrant families – there remains little difference in attitude towards girls and boys. Turkish daughters from first generation families are much burdened by additional duties in the household (such as buying household goods, cleaning, looking after younger brothers and sisters, cooking). Such duties are more onerous than in comparable families in Turkey and they increase especially when there are working opportunities for their mothers, which is more the case if mothers have at least some formal education. Though household participation of girls decreases in second generation families, it is still higher than that of boys, whose participation remains on the same (low) level and differs in no respect from that of similar German boys.

Intragenerational changes in Turkish migrant families

Empirical analyses on migration behaviour of Turkish men and women (Abanan-Unat, 1982) not only show that migrants are a selective population with respect to a longer formal education, higher occupational prestige, more urban background and a younger age than the average population of their country of origin, but these factors have a direct influence on the placement of migration in the life span, on the modalities of family migration succession and on later assimilation experience too. For example, migrant families from the modernized provinces of Turkey, from an urban environment and from families whose socialization is higher with weak religious bonds, with longer formal education and with neolocal settlement migrate earlier in their lives than do families with the opposite attributes. These factors also affect migration succession (i.e. whether family members migrate together or successively).

Families with male pioneer migrants form the main type of work migration (76.4 per cent). Families with female pioneer migrants (13.1 per cent) are barely more common than joint migrations (10.4 per cent). The same conditions that cause migration at a younger age also lead to a shortened period of separation, which consequently results in a tendency for 'early' and 'joint' migration to go together. Migration succession covers different periods of separation. While male chain migrants follow their wives after 3.5 years on average, female chain migrants rest in their country of origin for 4.6 years (i.e. in the case of female pioneers the tendency towards family reunion is stronger). The 'historic' conditions of migration succession have changed considerably in the last thirty years. While families with a first member migrating before 1962 remained separated for more than 10 years, the separation period has been reduced progressively to under 2 years for families who started their migration in the 1980s. This trend indicates the increasing importance of family considerations for migration decisions, considerations which evidently outweigh macrosocial conditions or political regulations.

Early childcare practices

The relationship between changing context opportunities and individual alternatives have been analysed in relation to early childcare practices in a survey of 520 migrant families.

● Childcare: 85 per cent of the children remained in their own nuclear family during their early childhood, all others stayed mainly with their relatives in Turkey (11 per cent). These proportions are independent of the native country of the child (i.e. families in Turkey often leave their children in the care of relatives as well).

- Regular medical examination during early childhood: 73 per cent of the parents say that the child has undergone regular medical examination, 12 per cent irregular, 11 per cent during illness and 3 per cent never.
- Breastfeeding: children are breastfed by Turkish mothers for 8.9 months on average. In Turkey boys are generally breastfed one month longer, in Germany one month shorter than girls.
- Regular feeding times: 62 per cent of the parents fed their child on regular time schedules, the others depending on circumstances (19 per cent) or when the child showed some demand (19 per cent).

In Germany regular feeding schedules are more frequent for boys than for girls (eta = .16), as opposed to Turkey, where there is no difference (eta = .04).

- Adherence to diet schedules: 57 per cent of parents conform 'very strictly' or 'mostly' to medical diet schedules when preparing food for their children.
- Toilet training: toilet training was completed for one half of the children after one-and-a-half years; for 11 per cent it lasted for more than 3 years, until the child did not need nappies any more. For children born in Germany, boys have more time to get used to toilets than girls (eta = .15), as opposed to Turkey, where there is no difference (eta = .03).
- Children's activity space: 12 per cent of Turkish parents had a child's bed in the form of a railed cot; 9 per cent had a playpen;15 per cent of children could move in one room during crawling age; 64 per cent of the children could move through out the whole appartment.

All variables which indicate individual alternatives for action, that is schooling, secularization (detachment from religious bonds to Islam, seen as restricting alternatives), cognitive assimilation (knowledge of the language of the 'host' society) and social assimilation (private contact with natives and participation in institutions of the 'host' society) point in the same direction:

- the longer the formal education, the looser the religious bonds, the higher the cognitive and social assimilation of Turkish mothers and fathers;

- the more often extrafamilial alternatives of care in early childhood are chosen;
- the more regular the medical examination of the child is;
- the shorter the breastfeeding period is;
- the more regular time schedules for feeding are used;
- the stricter medical diet schedules for the composition of meals are followed;
- the earlier toilet training is completed;
- the smaller is the children's action space during crawling age.

Table 9.1 Individual alternatives of Turkish male (M) and Female (F) migrants and early childcare

		school years	secularization	cognitive assimilation	social assimilation
extrafamilial	M	.05	.09	.11	.06
caretakers	F	.12	.12	.18	.13

The influence of individual alternatives on early childcare is stronger for mothers than for fathers, because their situation has changed more. So, the gain of individual alternatives for Turkish women is combined with a marked standardization of early childcare practices, which is guided by a balance between the needs of children and the needs of parents beyond educational tasks. The parental opportunities for a stronger situational control contain reductions of time-intensive care practices (breastfeeding; toilet training) as well as restrictions in the child's action space and more frequent use of extra-familial alternatives such as caretakers, medical controls and diet schedules, which may relieve mothering activities at least psychologically. Thus, an increase in individual alternatives leads to an economization of early childcare routines for Turkish migrant women in terms of parental costs (working costs are lower, but at least some financial costs are higher). As Table 9.1 also shows, the relationship between the various indicators of individual alternatives and early childcare does not always have the same intensity. As expected the weakest influence (according to accumulated research on assimilation processes) is religious bonds, the strongest influences are cognitive and social assimilation in the 'host' society. Concerning the latter, language abilities seem to be more important than close contacts with native persons.

Educational attitudes

In the same empirical study the educational attitudes during the assimilation process of Turkish parents are analysed: whether an obtained cognitive (language abilities), structural (housing and living comfort), and social (private contacts with natives and partic- ipation in institutions of the 'host' society) assimilation lead to changes in educational attitudes. For the measurement of educa- tional attitudes, five Turkish adaptations of (shortened) scales on self-perceived educational attitudes (Engfer and Schneewind, 1978) for the parent-child-dyads 'mother-daughter', 'mother-son', 'father-daughter' and 'father-son' were applied. The scales contain 'protectiveness' (tender, affective ties; over-protectiveness), 'authoritarian control' (non-compliant insistence on parental demands), 'conservatism' (orientation towards self-perceived education in own childhood), 'self-criticism' (perception of prob- lems, inconsistencies, lack of self-control in own educational behaviour), and 'permissiveness' (giving the child autonomy to make its own experience).

The disposition of protectiveness heads the hierarchy (x = 14.8). Whereas for Turkish mothers no sex-specific differentiation is noticeable, Turkish fathers protect their daughters more than their sons (p < .01). The disposition of authoritarianism follows with a marked distance (x = 12.3). Again Turkish mothers do not show sex-differentiation, while fathers are far more authoritarian towards their sons and less authoritarian towards their daughters than the mothers (p < .001). Their own education (x = 11.6) serves for mothers as well as for fathers more as a model for the education of daughters than for the education of sons (p < .01). Educational 'innovations' are more often applied to sons than to daughters, and they are more often encountered in mothers than in fathers. Strong differences are apparent with respect to educational self- reliance (x = 10.3). Self-criticism and erraticism is particularly frequent in the relationship between Turkish mothers and their daughters, much less in the relationship towards their sons (p < .001). Turkish fathers show high self-reliance towards their daugh- ters, more self-criticism in their relation to their sons (p < .01). With respect to the 'right' education for daughters there seem to be highly divergent concepts in Turkish migrant families. Permissiveness holds the last rank place in the educational atti- tudes under consideration (x = 10.2). As an inversion of the results on conservatism, mothers are much more permissive than fathers and permissiveness is more often shown towards sons than towards daughters (p < .001).

For an explanation of the rapid change in generative behaviour, early childcare practices, educational attitudes and socialization practices, some basic conditions of parent-child relationships in native Turkish families have to be taken into consideration (Kagitcibasi, 1982). In Turkish society a strong socio-structural differentiation in the value of children for their parents has been observed. In rural contexts and in families of low formal education the possession of (many) children is combined with strong economic-utilitarian benefits-expectations. There is an expectation of early help in household chores, of early work and additional contributions to the household income, and especially the expectation of later (economic) old age security. In urban contexts and in families with extended formal education, the possession of (few) children is combined with psychological-emotional benefits-expectations – the expectation of a strengthening of the affective ties within the family group and in the relationship of the spouses, and the expectation of expressive stimulation in interaction with children. These different expectations not only have drastic consequences for generative decisions, such as for many or few children and for a sex preference for (male) descendants, but also for the socialization of children.

The rank-order of educational dispositions and also the dyadic variations can easily be related to these basic assumptions. In the case of predominance of economic-utilitarian expectancy strong parental control convictions were expected (i.e. authoritarian rigidity as well as over-protectiveness but low permissiveness and low children's autonomy). But it has to be emphasized that this control (especially towards girls) is based far more on tender care, anxious protection and affective ties than on rigid insistence on instrumental parental norms. The relatively low educational traditionalism must also be emphasized. One's own education in the society of origin is rarely accepted by Turkish families as an adequate model under migrant conditions (especially for sons).

The explanation of changes in educational attitudes resulting from assimilation processes is based on the assumption that assimilation is combined with an enrichment of individual action alternatives – referring to the situation in the receiving society. Thus, the direction of change in educational attitudes will be identical to the direction of change brought about by formal education in the society of origin (i.e., economic-utilitarian expectations towards children will be reduced and psychological expectations will be increased). Accordingly, highly assimilated parents will value authoritarianism and protectiveness less and permissiveness more than poorly assimilated parents. Assimilation will also contribute to a rejection of self-perceived education as a model (i.e., assimilated parents will have fewer 'conservative' educational attitudes. At the same time, given individual alternatives will increase self-reliance in education (i.e. poorly assimilated parents will be much more 'self-critical' and uncertain in their educational attitudes).

Table 9.2 shows the correlations between formal education, assimilation and educational attitudes for all four parent-child dyads. The relationships – where they are significant – point in all dyads in the theoretically expected direction, which confirms the explanation with regard to the change of educational attitudes under migrant conditions. However, comparisons with the correlations to formal education (obtained in the society of origin), which itself is the major basis for assimilation, demonstrate that assimilation does not contribute much to attitude change: the correlations with 'formal education' are hardly lower than those with the 'assimilation'-variables. Attitude differences are most probably acquired to a great extent in the society of origin and 'imported' thereafter, and are not a result of culture contact.

A comparison of the dyads shows in detail that the mother-child relationships are much more 'stable' than father-child relationships and are not much affected by educational and assimilation processes. The longer the formal education and the assimilation, the more permissive and less authoritarian mothers become towards their daughters. In the case of their sons, only conservatism loses its importance. Fathers' educational attitudes are generally influenced far more by formal education and assimilation; whereas the relationship towards daughters is more affected by education, the relationship towards sons is affected more by assimilation. For the daughters, protectiveness remains high, while authoritarianism, conservatism and self-criticism are reduced and permissiveness increased with longer formal education. For the sons, even the extent of protectiveness is reduced with assimilation; but these fathers are not more permissive towards their sons – the correlations between assimilation and permissiveness are in this respect rather contradictory.

It may be of general importance for migration and family sociology that changes in the parent-child relationship are least influenced by structural placement in the receiving society (the

Table 9.2 Assimilation and educational attitudes in Turkish families

	formal education	cognitive	structural assimilation	social
mother-daughter				
protectiveness	−.04	−.01	−.20**	−.03
authoritarianism	−.19**	−.09	−.20**	−.19**
conservatism	−.01	.03	−.11	−.16*
self-criticism	−.14*	−.01	−.03	.09
permissiveness	.08	.17*	−.11	.20**
mother-son				
protectiveness	.06	−.04	−.17**	.07
authoritarianism	.07	−.08	−.04	.00
conservatism	−.23***	−.26***	−.02	−.22***
self-criticism	.01	.10	−.18**	.08
permissiveness	−.03	.03	.01	.03
father-daughter				
protectiveness	−.03	−.11*	.12*	−.04
authoritarianism	−.35***	−.19***	−.03	−.19***
conservatism	−.21***	−.16**	−.07	−.12*
self-criticism	−.20***	−.12*	.00	−.11*
permissiveness	.15**	.18**	.12*	.24***
father-son				
protectiveness	−.05	−.20***	−.08	−.14**
authoritarianism	−.13**	−.14**	−.09	−.17**
conservatism	−.02	−.01	.02	−.24***
self-criticism	−.14**	−.19***	−.05	−.16**
permissiveness	−.01	−.18**	.19***	−.12*

Note: * = p <.10; ** = p <.05; *** = p <.01

correlations with individual and family income and with occupational prestige are even weaker than with the index used, which measures possession of durable consumer goods and housing comfort). Changes are attributable to the enrichment of individual alternatives resulting mainly from an increase in individual competence (education, language acquisition) and social contacts (friends, participation) rather than in economic resources.

According to a 'situational' explanation of changes in migrant families, it is expected that socialization behaviour will change much more as a result of given individual alternatives in the receiving context than educational attitudes do. The individual alternatives in the assimilation process are analyzed according to formal education (EDUC); individual assimilation (cognitive assimilation, COGASS; structural assimilation, STRASS; social assimilation, SOCASS); position in the family life cycle at time of migration (MIGCYC) of Turkish women (F) and men (M), and early childcare practices (CARE). The migration cycle indicates the socialization in parental roles in the society of origin as well as to an important extent the parity, because high fertility appears mostly before migration. For the early childcare practices an index has been established, which measures the extent of 'rationality' according to the results of Table 9.3.

Table 9.3 Assimilation and socialization practices in Turkish migrant families

		FORMED	COGASS	STRASS	SOCASS	MIGCYC	CARE
Children's work	F	−.21	−.08		−.05	.18	
in the household	M	−.15	−.12	−.06	−.01	.19	−.15
Parents' activities	F	.26	.33		.33	−.23	
with the child	M	.23	.26	.14	.28	−.15	.26
Institutional	F	.30	.39		.37	−.19	
stimulation	M	.28	.31	.25	.27	−.10	.27
Religious	F	−.18	−.16		−.09	.15	
socialization	M	−.16	−.13	−.17	−.06	.11	−.14
Possession of Turkish	F	.12	.11		.10	.03	
children's books	M	.11	.19	.11	.12	.03	.05
Possession of German	F	.15	.29		.27	−.05	
children's books	M	.21	.34	.29	.20	−.02	.16
Consumption of	F	−.16	−.10		−.01	.23	
ethnic music	M	−.19	−.12	−.05	.01	.23	−.12
Consumption of	F	.19	.28		.26	−.07	
cosmopolitan music	M	.14	.23	.30	.18	−.01	.14

Children's help in household tasks is an aspect of family social-ization which is strongly associated with economic-utilitarian expectations towards children. In Turkish migrant families, the respective child buys food and household goods (47.9 per cent), helps with the cleaning (28.9 per cent), looks after younger broth-ers and sisters (24.2 per cent) and helps with the cooking (15.3 per cent) 'daily' or 'several times a week'. The correlation analysis shows that these kinds of children's work decrease according to the formal education of the parents and with increased rationaliza-tion in early childcare practices, and that children's work increases in families which migrate late in the family life cycle. This is related to the fact that high parity makes children's work in the household a necessity ($r = .28$), and not the extended stay (of the mother) in the society of origin ($r = .18$). Individual assimilation has no (reducing) effect on children's work in the household. Similar relationships are given with regard to the rigidity of religious socialization.

Active involvement of parents with children and the stimulation of children through extrafamilial institutions (besides school) are both aspects of familial socialization associated with psychological utility expectations towards children. Turkish parents control schoolwork 'daily' or 'several times a week' (17.5 per cent), read or tell stories to their child (7.9 per cent), engage in sports (4.8 per cent), sing with them (4.2 per cent) or practise a musical instru-ment together (3.8 per cent).

With regard to institutional stimulation parents report that 38.1 per cent of their children use public libraries, 30.6 per cent are members of a sports club, 11.7 per cent attend a music school, 10.4 per cent practise a musical instrument, 10.0 per cent attend a group for schoolwork assistance, 7.9 per cent receive private lessons, 6.2 per cent are members of a folk-dance group and 5.2 per cent receive full day child care outside the family. The correla-tion analysis shows relationships in the theoretically expected direction. With increasing individual alternatives (especially for the mother) parental activities with children are increased as well as their institutional stimulation. The effects of cognitive and social assimilation in the receiving society are more pronounced than those of formal education in the society of origin. Psychological utility expectations are mainly the result of assimilation processes and are not 'imported', as is true for economic-utilitarian expectan-cies. These conclusions are supported by the finding that parental activities and institutional stimulation are more related to (early) migration in the family life cycle of the women ($r = -.23/-.19$) and the rationalization of early childhood care ($r = .26/.27$) than to parity ($r = -.17/-.13$).

The possession of Turkish and German children's books and the children's consumption of ethnic and cosmopolitan music relate mainly to cultural ties resulting from family socialization. The possession of books may be judged to be an indicator of more prestigious (and more costly) cultural activities, while consumption of music is related more to popular culture. In general, Turkish youngsters possess more German than Turkish books (excluding school books) and listen more to cosmopolitan than to Turkish music: 48.1 per cent have no Turkish, 40.0 per cent no German books, 13.4 per cent have more than 10 Turkish books and 32.8 per cent more than 10 German books. According to the answers of their parents, the child listens 'daily' or 'several times a week' to popular Arab music (36.3 per cent), Turkish arranged popular music (31.9 per cent), Turkish folklore (24.4 per cent) and classical Turkish music (12.1 per cent), as well as to contemporary Turkish music (4.4 per cent), Western classical music (4.9 per cent), German pop songs (38.8 per cent) and international pop and rock music (40.4 per cent). The correlation analysis shows that the action alternatives achieved by education and assimilation do not result in loss of options on (prestigious aspects of) culture of origin or on minority culture, respectively, and substitution by options on the culture of the majority. Instead, the contingency of marginal existence and a large number of individual alternatives lead to double options rather than to 'clear decisions'. The possession of Turkish children's books also increases with the formal education of the parents and their assimilation. Regarding the more 'trivial' consumption of music, one can observe a relatively early rejection of ethnic popular music (folklore) and Arab popular music and a strong commitment to international pop music, depending on the educational level of the parents; the same, however, is true for German youngsters. In general, the correlation analysis demonstrates that socialization practices change more with the assimilation process and the increased action alternatives than do educational attitudes.

Conclusion

These empirical results are well able to correct some of the existing black-and-white pictures and stereotypes and the flirtations with exotic folkloristic presentations, which have dominated (presumably, not only German) application-oriented discussion on minority education, the legal position of foreigners and social work. Even in well-meaning literature such minorities are preferably portrayed as strongly structured by ritualistically obeyed social norms, invariably captive to doctrinal or irrational traditions, and as unconsciously facing one culture shock after another in their struggle to come to terms with the 'host' society

The results of empirical research reveal another picture, which stresses in particular the high variability within migrant families. In a cross-cultural comparative perspective, German families are much more homogeneous in their performance, attitudes and behaviour than Turkish families or Turkish migrant families. In several respects, Turkish urban families much more resemble German families than they do their East Anatolian counterparts. Furthermore, empirical results are impressive in showing the high capacity of migrant families for adaptation and reorganization when facing new socio-ecological contingencies and changing development tasks in the family life cycle. These intrafamilial changes can be explained adequately as the result of rational behavioural strategies, even if constraints are at times very strong.

10

MUSLIM COMMUNITIES, ETHNIC MINORITIES AND CITIZENS

DOMINIQUE SCHNAPPER

Although not all the immigrants from former colonial empires or the southern hemisphere that have settled in Western Europe since World War II are Muslim, the majority of them are. But it is not just a question of number. The uncertainties, the anxieties and the – sometimes violent – opposition that newcomers invariably awaken crystallize round the presence of Muslims. Misgivings are felt both about their commitment to modern democratic societies and about their ability to integrate into European nations. In particular, perhaps two features of Muslim tradition make such commitment difficult, some would say impossible. The practice of Islam goes beyond the strictly religious domain, religious laws compel recognition in every aspect of social and personal life. Put differently, religious issues are not separated from social and political issues, whereas modern societies take freedom of expression as axiomatic. Then Muslim tradition reserves a particular place for women, whereas equality for all, for women as for men, is both a principle and a passion in modern democracies. Moreover, it may be questioned whether the democratic nations of Western Europe have retained the values and institutions that are capable of enabling such newcomers to integrate.

In former times, doctors and exponents of Muslim law found themselves able by learned and subtle argument to adapt it to different historical circumstances. In the name of *darūra*, necessity, they found it possible to authorize and justify an accommodation enabling the faithful settled in non-Muslim lands to break with the letter of certain practices, while still continuing to be recognized as Muslim. Certain verses in the Qur'an had already made provision for circumstances in which some things, in principle forbidden, might be allowed if necessary. Like all the great sacred texts, the Qur'an is susceptible to reinterpretation in accordance with the demands made on the lives of individuals and groups (Lewis Chapter 1).

But the exponents of the law have so far not dealt with a problem that has no precedent in history, the problem of relations between Muslims and non-Muslims in a situation brought about not by necessity but by the exodus of a Muslim minority, who left of their own will and settled in non-Muslim countries. Today Muslim intellectuals in Europe are faced with the task of setting the terms of a necessary compromise between faith and participation in communal life and of conceiving how Islam can be made compatible with the demands of a society which is by definition secular, while guaranteeing freedom of religious belief and practice.

During our survey, we frequently encountered remarks similar to that of the young Muslim, quoted by Bernard Lewis: 'my father was a Muslim, but I am a Parisian.' Such an assertion, however illogical, sums up nonetheless a common experience, commitment to a new 'homeland' (in fact local rather than national) superimposed on the reference to Islam.

Clearly it remains a fact that the settlement of Muslims in non-sectarian Europe with its Christian tradition is bound to give rise to problems and conflict that cannot be written off simply as the effect of racial prejudice on the part of Europeans. This is particularly the case since, as Johannes Jansen (Chapter 3) and Bernard Lewis (Chapter 1) remind us, the Christian imagination is rich in fantastical representations of Islam, perceived as irrational, fanatical, violent and dangerous. But at least the essentialist picture of Islam as one and immutable needs exploding. Muslims in Europe who practise or look to Islam are as varied in their social and national affiliations as in their manner of living through and submitting to Islam. The Islam of the French Maghrebins is not the same as that of the Pakistanis in Britain, the Turks in Germany or the Moroccans, Turks and natives of Surinam and the Moluccas in the Netherlands.

The diversity of experience stems also from policy differences between European countries, reflecting their respective experience of how integration has been applied. At first sight these policies appear to diverge considerably. For example, Germany and Switzerland have endeavoured to apply a policy of *Gastarbeiter*, guest workers, whose engagement is provisional as their task is limited. Conversely, France, which has fostered immigration for nearly two centuries, has continued to apply a policy of integration (for a long time described as assimilation) in respect of foreigners who take up residence legitimately, turning migrants – or at any rate their children – into French citizens. The Netherlands and Sweden, with their liberal traditions, initially practised a policy of respecting particular identities and recognizing communities within the public arena. Britain tends to have a similar objective, but the Jacobin tradition in France precludes this. Such differences apart, there are signs at present of increasing convergence between the policies in force in different European countries and the development of the Muslim populations there.

Until the recent arrival of Turks and Black Africans, the vast majority of Muslims in France were of Maghrebin extraction, in particular Algerian. Islam of the Maghreb has among its ingredients, traces of the Roman presence, Kabyl and Berber tradition, the characteristics common to all Mediterranean countries, and of course the long-standing influence of the French who, in the case of Algeria, were settled there for more than a century. Hence the debate on polygamy, and on welfare rights associated with it, in the Netherlands affects only a small fraction of the Muslim population in France and Britain, recent immigrants from Black Africa. On the other hand, for Pakistanis the link between religion and national identity in their homeland – Pakistan separated from union with India over the question of Islam – has an effect on the politicization of Pakistanis in Britain (Werbner, Chapter 7).

In some cases, immigrants have come from backward rural regions and are still little adapted to the modern conditions of living to which they aspire. In others, they represent highly cultured urban populations. This is the case with Pakistanis in Britain. Economically, they are highly successful and they suffer from the disparity between their economic success and their paltry political role.

Much emigration is the legacy of colonialism and the end of empire, counting for the major part in the case of Britain and about half in that of France and the Netherlands. Inevitably, relations between both parties – one-time colonizers and the colonized – bear the marks of history. Their colonial policies were different. In the main, the British made a point of administering indirect or home rule, in other words consolidating power at a local level and overseeing traditional chiefs and leaders, the source of whose authority thus became the colonial power. The treatment of Jamaicans or Indians, now resident and naturalized in Britain, is in keeping with the historical context. The British conceive of relations between groups in terms of 'race', level accusations of racialism at one another (Husband, chapter 6), and tend to group immigrant populations in communities, represented by commissions, so extending the practice of indirect rule.

The Dutch considered their colonies chiefly as a source of economic exploitation. They worked on the principle of respecting local customs. Moreover they were not concerned to introduce European values and institutions, nor even to generalize their own language. The same intention of respecting particular forms of culture informed immigrant policy until the beginning of the 1980s. A change of approach then came about when it was observed that many of those who came from Surinam and the Moluccas, most of them of Dutch nationality and in any event all bound to remain in the Netherlands, were without the cultural means to escape unemployment or marginalization.

Approaching the problem in a quite different way, the French made it their business to spread their culture throughout their colonies, in line with the civilizing mission it represented. A policy of assimilation was implemented overseas, just as in France in respect of the children of immigrants. The policy of integration at an individual not collective or 'community' level remains an intrinsic part of the 'Republican compact.' However, the memory of colonial relations and the violence of the struggle for independence have dramatized relations between the Maghrebin and the local population.

Muslims do not form a political community in Britain, but Pakistanis who are frequently concentrated in urban areas, organized in religious communities by their more active members, and grouped close to their mosque which serves as a nucleus for the community, enjoy a degree of cultural and institutional autonomy that is unknown elsewhere in Europe, and their communal life is active and busy. So far they lack some of the rights accorded to other religions where schools are concerned. Nevertheless they have their own radio and television programmes and their requests for more mosques are acceded to, judging by the number being built. Their disapproval of what they see as too much freedom in

Western customs has resulted in their often being allowed to
exempt girls in primary and secondary schools from classes or
activities judged improper (biology, physical education, dancing,
swimming) or to bend uniform rules in their favour (headscarves,
arm and leg covering). In addition, school timetables allow for
their feast days and school meals for their dietary arrangements.
Since the start of the Salman Rushdie affair, Pakistanis have had no
hesitation in taking a political stand, frankly and closely linked to
their adherence to Islam. They openly defy the principle of religious neutrality and the loosening of moral standards in the West,
and they openly and collectively showed their opposition to British
policy at the time of the Gulf War (Werbner, Chapter 7). At the
close of 1991, some called for a 'Muslim Parliament', a political
body to speak for Muslims as such. The ethnic furthering of political and social life hand in hand with the notion of minorities,
whose rights must be recognized, provides the dominant model
for intergroup relationships, a model that is fundamentally
opposed to the French one of integration. One only has to glance
at the contributions here from British colleagues to be aware of the
extent to which Pakistanis in Britain think in terms of 'community'
and 'race' and 'racialism', whereas for the French citizenship
continues to be the cementing factor.

In the Netherlands, mention has been made of the policy of
respect for identities being called into question early in the 1980s.
Terrorist activities on the part of youths of Moluccan extraction
drew attention to the fact that the immigrants were there to stay
and further that those of the second generation who attended
school knew insufficient Dutch to be able to find work. It was thus
decided to implement a joint 'policy of integration and protection
of separate identity'. Integration in the Netherlands rests on a
political contract, which sets up a form of collaboration between
the three mainstay institutions – the Catholic and Protestant
churches and the secularized state. Each has its own schools,
hospitals, housing schemes, unions, welfare associations, sports
clubs and radio stations. There is little contact between the three,
but the élites provide communal life with a structure and coalesce
the different elements into a system which is given unified expression by the notion of nationhood. Muslims have obtained some of
the rights appertaining to the three institutionalized bodies. For
instance, there are some Muslim primary schools and special
programmes on radio and television. The imams who are trained
and directed by their Turkish and Moroccan authorities are recog-

nized as religious leaders. It is accepted that welfare cover may be extended to polygamy. But the policy increasingly comes up against abuses on the part of families, the spread of fundamentalism, the hold that the Turkish and Moroccan governments still exercise over their nationals, the refusal, for example, for Turks and Moroccans to be assimilated into Dutch society, and the lack of coherence in the programme of 'heritage' languages and culture, which all parties recognize as having failed but no politician has the courage to do away with. Now the Dutch government is applying a so-called integration policy, implying that cultural identity of immigrants is taken account of insofar as it does not hamper their participation in Dutch society. But the effects of this new policy will not be felt for some time.

A policy of individual integration, customary in a country with an 'open door' tradition and in keeping with Jacobin notions of citizenship, continues to operate in France for all who belong to the higher social categories. Such people are French in all but name and see themselves as citizens in the full sense, maintaining only token and intermittent – essentially sentimental – links with their homeland. They have no wish to win public acceptance for some form of 'Muslim' or 'Arab community'. This was earlier implied by their refusal to be drawn into the Rushdie affair and given further substance by their attitude during the Gulf War. As the crisis unfolded, they received the impression that they were being put to the test and suspected of 'divided loyalty'. In particular, they were shocked that the President of the Republic could allude to the existence of an 'Arab community' when they felt themselves to be 'no different' from other citizens. If, as a result of what they were made to go through, many decided to vote differently, there were no misgivings about French citizenship as such, nor about integration as being an individual and not a community concern (Rachedi, Chapter 5). Nor do other social categories exhibit Maghrebin or Muslim culture.

Children of immigrants sent to school in France display the same knowledge, the same tastes and attitudes as do other children from comparable backgrounds, and they do not appear to hanker after some or other form of community. Promulgating this is left to individuals working from outside. A few minority members of the Maghrebin élite seek recognition from the government as 'authorized intermediaries'. In the suburbs, which are deeply unsettled by the disintegration of the working class, Muslim fundamentalists, in most cases coming from abroad, endeavour to bring young people who are marginalized and unable, with unemployment rife, to find their place in French society back into the fold. The government has sought a remedy by setting up a body modelled on the Jewish Assemblies or Protestant Federation to provide a forum for problems relating to Muslim life and practice, a difficult assignment given the diversity of population. Paradoxically, the state which is unitary and non-sectarian cannot treat Islam other than as a religion. But in any event there is neither evidence of the existence of a specific culture nor of community aspiration, merely of various forms of political strategy designed to further Muslim interests on the part of a number of individuals working within the French system. Ethnic consciousness for its own sake or fostered in the form of a 'community' is not, at least not for the moment, a concrete reality (Roy, Chapter 4).

In spite these wide divergences in policy, the case of Germany shows that evolution on the ground shows less divergence than is claimed both in speeches and in policy as advocated and applied. France offers a very 'open' body of law relating to nationality, giving considerable latitude to *jus soli*, in a way that allows room for the political integration of immigrants. In particular, Article 44 allows children born in France to parents who are themselves foreign to become naturalized when they are eighteen, if they have not renounced the right during the year preceding their majority and if they have lived in France during the five years preceding their majority. Sweden, the Netherlands and Belgium have recently altered their naturalization laws in this direction. Britain, too, under certain conditions allows such children to become naturalized.

On other hand, German nationality continues to be based in the first instance on blood ties (*jus sanguinis*). Nationality can only be acquired by becoming naturalized. Foreign children have no automatic or semi-automatic right to nationality, even when they are born and have received their schooling in Germany. This results in the situation of foreigners, who have settled in Germany and may well be culturally German, finding it extremely difficult to become naturalized, whereas the grandchildren of expatriates from Silesia, Pomerania or the Volga, who may be unable to speak German, are welcomed as nationals. This is why Friedrich Heckmann (Chapter 8) dwells on the fact that the attitude of the Germans, springing from a concept of the nation that is not political but primarily biological and ethnic, tends to exclude foreigners. The practice with *Gastarbeiter* adhered to this tradition: workers needed to sustain economic development were recruited to undertake precise tasks for a limited period of time; there was no question of their becoming German. But once such people have settled in for a generation or more, the practice is likely to lead to Muslims forming political minorities, which are culturally assimilated but deprived of citizens' rights.

Nevertheless, the close, precise surveys carried out by Bernhard Nauck (Chapter 9) show that the Turks, though their children are barred from acquiring German nationality, nonetheless experience a transformation that affects every detail of family life. Even though they are victims of 'structural' hostility, as sociologists term it, in fact they become culturally integrated and increasingly take on the values, norms and attitudes prevailing in German society, which are also those of the present day. It is true that the number of marriages between Turks and Germans shows little increase in the second generation, and burials still take place in the home country, because the Turks form a minority community in Germany. But fertility among Turkish women who have grown up and been to school in Germany is on a level with that of German women rather than with their compatriots who have never left home. The principles guiding their education, showing greater latitude and concern for individuality, are now far more in line with what society as a whole expects.

In France too official statistics make it clear that fertility among women of immigrant stock is falling into line with patterns in the majority, that the number of marriages between foreigners and French nationals is on the increase, and that a majority of immigrants experience a degree of social mobility which is comparable with that of French people from similar backgrounds. It has to be borne in mind that, with the exception of political exiles, immigrants are generally speaking younger, better educated and in the main more urbanized than are their parents' generation. In addition, they are driven by the urge to emigrate and to achieve social mobility.

European societies are developing ever closer characteristics. Political or democratic intensions are less articulate than is the general desire to participate in economic activity and enjoy equality in education, living conditions and employment, as well as the benefits of social welfare. It is through the operation of social and economic policy and in ways that differ between one European country and another that government achieves the integration of the various groups, including immigrants. The state has come to

have the function of regulating the social compact. By its action it
ensures the organization of the major public services – education,
amenities, urban and housing development, regulates conflicts that
arise between the different parties to economic activity, and
provides for a degree of social redistribution through the mecha-
nism of transfer expenditure. Immigrants, who have the same
claim on welfare as nationals, benefit from such action and achieve
gradual integration because they participate in economic activity
and are given welfare cover. But this has neither the same meaning
nor the same effect as integration achieved through sharing the
same political values. When difficulties arise due to the economic
recession and, in particular, high unemployment, the process of
integration may well face dramatic reversal; and indeed unemployment appears to have taken on permanency in Europe.

Every European country pledges itself to freedom of expression
and worship, from which follows the pluralistic nature of society.
But this secular principle gives rise to divergent relationships
between organized religion and the state. Religions are sometimes
recognized by law, as in Switzerland or Germany. The British
sovereign is head of the Anglican Church. Islam has penetrated
schools in Britain, where the day begins with a gathering for
prayers. In Belgium, Germany and Switzerland, religious education, funded by the state, is dispensed within the state schools
system. Even in France, where attachment to the secular principle
is most closely associated with political tradition, where the separation between church and state was proclaimed with greater vehemence than elsewhere, and where education is 'national' and
non-sectarian, religious bodies have devised particular relationships with the state and managed to negotiate terms for religious
teaching and for the observance of feast days and ceremonies.
Given that they have the means of playing an active part in
economic and social life, Muslims have no reason not to settle in a
democracy and establish durable relations with government just as
other religions do, but on the understanding that they agree to
redefine Islam as a religion on a par with other religions. Whatever
the relationship between the state and a religious body amounts to
in practice, the principle of neutrality requires in every instance
that Islam is regarded as a religion and that it no longer is, whether
for community or individual, an all-embracing way of life. So long
as their practice conforms to their declared principles, liberal
democracies can integrate the faithful of whatever creed and religion, provided the faithful abide by the law and the principles the
state upholds, including that of freedom of expression.

This is not to imply that this process does and will take place without conflict. Throughout Europe there are identical fantasies in regard to Islam and fundamentalism. Everywhere – and this is probably inevitable in liberal societies – abuses exist in obtaining welfare rights. Further, the memory of colonialism and the end of empire continues to trouble interrelationships. No country is free of the hostility shown to groups of newcomers that one knows as 'racialism'. Different types of 'nativist' movement, to use the American term, whereby the original values, real or reconstituted, are evoked and newcomers rejected in the name of these values, have always existed, even in countries founded on immigration like the USA, Australia or Argentina. Today such movements exist in all European countries, finding expression either in the rise of right-wing extremism or sporadic displays of social violence.

Whatever public claims are made for it as one religion among others, it will not be easy in European countries for Islam to make this transformation. The question may be asked whether Muslims are prepared to take so radical a step in the face of their tradition: there is no simple or single answer. Clearly Maghrebins in France differ in their attitude from Pakistanis in Britain. Even in the Netherlands, where national traditions are extremely liberal and where the political compact associates Protestants, Catholics and the non-sectarian element, Muslims are unable to gain recognition as a further interest group; material resources, power and prestige are too unequally distributed, the colonial past and Islam accord ill with national history. Parity between constituent groups, which provides the basis for integration in the older nations of Europe, is always forged across a long history.

Further to this, everywhere in Europe religions have adopted a low profile, churches intervene less in social affairs, ecclesiastical buildings are required to be lower than others, (in the Netherlands), religious practice dwindles, the outward and visible forms of belief give way to a religion that is more personal and more emotive. A conflict arising from the fact that gays and practising Muslims were both housed in the same council flats, or another because the animal rights lobby in the Netherlands showed offence at halal methods of slaughtering are not merely anecdotes. One wonders how readily Europeans can accept the visible expression of a constricting religion, as Islam is, when their own standards of behaviour are increasingly permissive and free of any reference to the teachings of organized religion.

It is no accident that, in every European country, the building of

mosques, whereby Islam is visibly recorded in a landscape traditionally organized around churches of different denominations,
and the education reserved for girls – because it is in schools that
traditionalist Muslims concentrate their efforts to enforce their
system of morality and transmit their identity – occasion the most
violent conflicts. In the Netherlands as in France or Britain, wearing the 'Islamic headscarf' in school takes on symbolic value.

The centuries-old history of relations between Christianity and
Islam and the more recent history of colonialism, still very much
part of people's consciousness, necessarily form a background to
relations between Muslims and non-Muslims. European countries
are traversing an economic recession that shows little sign of
easing and that is causing the number of unemployed – hence of
those excluded – to rise. But European countries are also experiencing a political crisis which affects their perception of their own
identity and the present structure of democracy itself, a crisis
rendered all the starker because the erstwhile common enemy –
communism – whose presence was a factor of cohesion is no
longer there.

Britain itself is facing a crisis of identity linked with the end of
empire and entry into the European Community (Husband,
Chapter 6). There is nothing exceptional in this. The colonial
empires of other European powers were less extensive than the
British Commonwealth, and Continental countries, properly
speaking, have perhaps come round more easily to the European
idea than the UK, whose ties with the USA and certain dominions
were close and complex. But all European nations are facing the
same crisis. Indeed, with the ending of the drive for conquest and
the fast-developing scale of interchange in population, products,
capital and information across national frontiers, given the fact of
increasing interdependence and the global transmission of ideas
and of models that are no longer the perquisite of any one nation,
one may well ask what meaning to give to membership of one
particular nation, or to the concept of nation itself. The building of
the European Community makes the crisis the more acute in that
the idea of nationhood was born in Europe. In these circumstances
a glib way out of the problem for many is to shift responsibility for
the crisis on to foreigners, and especially Muslims. For it would be
hardly surprising if the crisis of national identity did not provide an
occasion to 'ethnicize', both in name and substance, social and
political problems that follow from the demise of traditional working-class culture, the development of unemployment and the
wider sources of self-questioning.

Nevertheless, in democratic societies which uphold the rule of law, the only possible course is to endeavour to bring all sections of the population into the community and into the political process, whatever their origin and their religious faith. Economic and cultural integration is already a fact for a growing portion of the immigrant population whose schooling has taken place in Europe. Increasing numbers of Muslims are found, and will continue to be found, in the professions, in university teaching, in the media and in industry. Their social and cultural attributes differentiate them from their kin and make them indistinguishable from those they associate with; and resentment is felt that they continue to be underrepresented in public life (Husband, Chapter 6). But one needs rather to address the significance of their as yet early presence in politics. Several hundred French of Maghrebin extraction are now municipal councillors and they refuse to see themselves confined to 'immigrant' problems, declaring themselves no different from other French citizens. The election in Britain in 1987 of four members of parliament from ethnic minorities has symbolic value for those who originate from former colonies and are now British citizens. One wonders whether in Britain, where 'ethnic' consciousness is strong, they will act as enablers for 'coloured' people to play a part in the democratic process and so integrate fully, or whether they will serve to perpetuate a political tradition, which until now has denied them and their fellows positions of responsibility.

Given the different forms of national integration, the specific features of Moslem integration, as of national integration in general, are likely to persist for some time to come. But European construction is bound to impose a degree of harmonization in legislation governing the problem of immigration (including right of asylum) and in respect of nationality. It will become c cult to refuse rights in one European nation which have b accorded in another. In the long term, the Germans will be obli to give a more liberal interpretation to their own nationality just as Belgium and the Netherlands have done. The Scher agreement may well mark the first stage in the process of brin the different bodies of legislation into line.

Integration is both a political and a social necessity, since e thing must be done to avoid the formation of urban ghettos, of poverty, exclusion and ethnic apprehension, where, as in ce sectors of American cities, social and ethnic disadvantages compounded. But integration is foremost a value *per se*, inso it rests on the fundamentally democratic notion that, in spite of the divergence of their beliefs and their experience and their allegiances, people who have respect for what is right and, in particular, for human rights can live in harmony. This never meant they would be free of conflict, it meant acceptance on their part that conflicts can be resolved in accordance with rules they all accept. Muslims must observe the norms that regulate communal life. But, on their side, the democracies of Western Europe will be able to resolve the problems posed by the Muslim presence only by remaining loyal to the values to which they lay claim.

STATISTICAL APPENDIX

TABLE 1
TOTAL POPULATION AND LABOUR FORCE IN THE TWELVE COUNTRIES OF THE EC IN 1987

	Nationals + Foreigners			Foreigners only			% foreigners	
	Total pop. (× 1000)	Lab. force (× 1000)	wk. rate (%)	Total pop. (× 1000)	Lab. force (× 1000)	wk. rate (%)	Tot. pop. (%)	Lab. force (%)
	(1)	(2)	(3)	(4)	(5)	(6)	(7)	(8)
GERMANY	60 215	28 505	54.7	4629	2336	64.6	7.7	8.2
BELGIUM	9 789	3 914	48.3	801	289	47.6	8.2	7.4
DENMARK	5 093	2 801	65.9	78	45	69.3	1.5	1.6
SPAIN	38 298	14 270	46.8	113	44	45.7	0.3	0.3
FRANCE	53 421	23 970	55.8	3755	1526	56.2	7.0	6.4
GREECE	9 714	3 884	49.6	64	24	43.8	0.7	0.6
IRELAND	3 480	1 323	52.2	77	33	50.2	2.2	2.5
ITALY	56 399	23 138	49.2	–	–	–	–	–
LUXEMBURG	363	158	51.6	95	49	64.6	26.2	31.0
NETHERLANDS	14 297	6 500	55.2	531	223	55.1	3.7	3.4
PORTUGAL	10 214	4 704	57.7	50	17	49.4	0.5	0.4
UNITED KINGDOM	56 099	27 889	60.4	2409	1263	59.3	4.3	4.5

Total population

	Foreigners			Foreigners only			% foreigners	
	Total pop. (× 1000)	Lab. force (× 1000)	wk. rate (%)	Total pop. (× 1000)	Lab. force (× 1000)	wk. rate (%)	Tot. pop. (%)	Lab. force (%)
	(1)	(2)	(3)	(4)	(5)	(6)	(7)	(8)
				Women only:				
GERMANY	31 446	11 272	41.0	2131	764	46.6	6.8	6.8
BELGIUM	5 010	1 507	36.0	372	85	30.8	7.4	5.6
DENMARK	2 573	1 290	59.5	37	21	66.2	1.4	1.6
SPAIN	19 664	4 693	29.6	63	17	31.8	0.3	0.4
FRANCE	27 662	10 386	46.0	1774	474	37.7	6.4	4.6
GREECE	5 010	1 392	34.0	34	7	31.7	0.7	0.5
IRELAND	1 733	434	34.0	40	10	34.4	2.3	2.3
ITALY	29 056	8 228	53.6	–	–	–	–	–
LUXEMBURG	186	56	35.2	49	19	48.8	26.3	33.9
NETHERLANDS	7 217	2 445	40.9	240	54	31.0	3.3	2.2
PORTUGAL	5 314	1 968	45.7	26	6	33.7	0.5	0.3
UNITED KINGDOM	28 750	11 760	49.2	1242	532	47.9	4.3	4.5

Sources: For the first six columns: *Survey of Labour forces, Data 1987*, Luxemburg, Official Publications office of the European communities, 1989 [Table 1 for columns (1) to (3), Table 12 for column (4), Table 16 for column (5), Table 5 for column (6)]; column (7) = 100 × column (4)/column (1); column (8) = 100 × column (5)/column (2)

TABLE 2
GERMANY: INFORMATION AVAILABLE ON NUMBERS OF FOREIGNERS (A)

	1983	1984	1985	1986	1987	1988	1989	dont femme
FRANCE	71.9	72.4	74.8	76.7	78.7	71.8	77.6	–
GREECE	292.3	287.1	280.6	278.5	279.5	274.8	293.6	134.1
ITALY	565.0	545.1	531.3	537.1	544.4	508.7	519.5	207.1
NETHERLANDS	108.6	108.6	108.4	109.0	109.3	96.9	101.2	–
PORTUGAL	99.5	83.0	77.0	78.2	79.2	71.1	74.9	35.8
SPAIN	166.0	158.8	152.8	150.5	147.1	126.4	127.0	57.7
UNITED KINGDOM	88.0	87.3	88.1	90.0	92.1	83.0	85.7	–
OTHER EC	41.3	42.0	43.6	44.7	46.8	43.2	45.9	–
TOTAL EC (b)	1432.6	1384.3	1356.6	1364.7	1377.5	1275.9	1325.4	–
AUSTRIA	171.6	172.1	172.5	174.6	177.0	155.1	171.1	76.4
TURKEY	1552.3	1425.8	1401.9	1434.3	1481.4	1523.7	1612.6	743.8
YUGOSLAVIA	612.8	600.3	591.0	591.2	597.6	579.1	610.5	281.6
BULGARIA	4.1	4.1	4.3	4.5	4.7	–		–
POLAND	87.6	95.9	104.8	116.9	142.2	171.5	220.4	–
RUMANIA	12.3	12.8	13.7	15.0	17.5	–	–	–
SOVIET UNION	6.5	6.6	6.7	7.1	8.1	–	–	–
CZECHOSLOVAKIA	26.9	27.7	28.2	29.1	30.4	–	–	–
HUNGARY	21.1	21.1	21.4	23.1	25.8	–	–	–

TABLE 3
FRANCE: INFORMATION AVAILABLE ON NUMBERS OF FOREIGNERS

	1975	1982	1985	women only
ALGERIA	710.7	805.1	820.9[a]	338.3[a]
ITALY	462.9	340.3	277.1	122.9
MOROCCO	260.0	441.3	516.4	222.8
PORTUGAL	758.9	767.3	751.3	359.7
SPAIN	497.5	327.2	267.9	127.8
TUNISIA	139.7	190.8	202.6	84.4
TURKEY	50.9	122.3	146.1	68.3
YUGOSLAVIA	70.3	62.5	–	–
OTHER	491.5	657.4	769.9	359.6
TOTAL	3442.4	3714.2	3752.2	1683.8

(a) This estimate which is difficult to compare with the censuses of 1975 and 1982 includes, in the case of Algerians, children born in France to Algerian parents (about 290.000, of whom 142 000 were female) who in the eyes of the *Code de la Nationalité* are French; though Algeria considers them to be Algerian.

Sources. 1975 and 1982 INSEE (central statistical office), population census of 20/2/1975 and of 4/3/1982. For 1985, estimate by INED (National Institute of Demographic Studies) on 1/1/1986

TABLE 4
NETHERLANDS: INFORMATION AVAILABLE ON NUMBERS OF FOREIGNERS (a)

	1983	1984	1985	1986	1987	1988	1989	women only
BELGIUM	23.7	23.6	22.8	23.0	22.9	23.1	23.3	11.8
GERMANY	44.8	44.8	41.0	40.4	39.4	40.3	41.8	19.7
GREECE	4.0	4.0	3.8	3.8	4.0	4.3	4.5	1.6
ITALY	20.9	20.3	17.8	17.0	15.9	16.0	16.7	5.4
PORTUGAL	7.8	7.9	7.5	7.5	7.8	8.0	8.0	3.6
SPAIN	21.6	20.7	19.0	18.2	17.6	17.4	17.4	7.5
UNITED KINGDOM (b)	40.8	40.7	38.5	38.0	37.1	37.4	37.5	15.5
OTHER E.C.	10.2	10.6	11.1	11.8	12.2	13.3	13.5	6.6
TOTAL E.C. (c)	173.8	172.6	161.5	159.7	156.9	159.8	162.7	71.7
MOROCCO	106.4	111.3	116.4	122.7	130.1	139.2	148.0	65.8
TUNISIA	2.8	2.8	2.6	2.6	2.6	2.7	2.4	0.8
TURKEY	155.3	155.6	156.4	160.6	167.3	176.5	191.5	87.7
UNITED STATES	10.0	10.4	10.5	10.4	10.4	10.8	10.5	...
YUGOSLAVIA	12.7	12.2	11.7	11.6	11.7	12.1	12.8	6.0
OTHER	91.4	93.8	93.4	100.4	112.8	122.6	114.0	55.8
TOTAL	552.4	558.7	552.5	568.0	591.8	623.7	641.9	287.8
Women Only	237.8	241.1	239.8	249.2	260.5	277.2	287.8	

(a) number figuring on municipal registers on 31 December of each year
(b) including Hong-Kong
(c) This total includes Greece, Spain and Portugal for all years under consideration
Source: (Dutch) Central Statistical office

TABLE 5
GERMANY: NATURALIZATIONS ACCORDING TO COUNTRY OF FORMER NATIONALITY

	1987		1988	
	Total	%	Total	%
AUSTRIA	730	5.2	744	1.5
CZECHOSLAVAKIA	490	3.5	603	3.6
ITALY	538	3.8	607	3.6
POLAND	1 016	7.5	1 764	10.6
ROMANIA	230	1.6	199	3.0
HUNGARY	622	4.4	558	3.3
TURKEY	1 175	8.4	1 225	7.4
YUGOSLAVIA	1 913	13.6	1 734	10.1
OTHER EUROPEAN	1 308	9.3	–	–
INDIA	213	1.7	–	–
IRAN	272	1.9	–	–
KOREA	310	2.2	–	–
PHILIPPINES	574	4.1	–	–
SYRIA	296	2.1	–	–
AFRICA	905	6.5	–	–
AMERICAS	497	3.5	–	–
STATELESS	1 064	7.6	–	–
OTHER	1 816	12.9	8 926	53.6
TOTAL (a)	14 029	100.0	16 660	100.0

(a) only includes naturalizations obtained by means of a discretionary decision. The overall figures 37.810 in 1987 and 46.783 in 1988 – are obtained by the addition of naturalizations acquired by the normal criteria.
Source: Federal statistical office

TABLE 6

FRANCE: NATURALIZATIONS ACCORDING TO COUNTRY OF FORMER NATIONALITY

	1988		1989	
	Total	%	Total	%
ITALY	3 081	6.6	2 576	5.2
SPAIN	4 460	9.6	3 320	6.7
PORTUGAL	7 984	17.2	7 027	14.2
POLAND	1 298	2.8	1 587	3.2
TURKEY	690	1.5	921	1.9
YUGOSLAVIA	1 015	2.2	1 249	2.5
ALGERIA	3 256	7.0	4 070	8.3
MOROCCO	4 435	9.6	5 393	10.9
TUNISIA	2 317	5.1	2 538	5.1
CAMBODIA	1 511	3.3	1 724	3.5
LAOS	1 294	2.8	1 305	2.6
VIETNAM	2 012	4.3	2 478	5.0
OTHER	12 968	28.0	15 142	30.7
TOTAL (a)	46 351	100.0	49330	100.0

(a) Excluding children who became French by virtue of their parents obtaining French nationality, ie 7948 in 1988 and 10178 in 1989. Naturalizations only constitute one of the means of acquiring French nationality. Every year roughly 120,000 persons acquire French nationality

Source: Department of Population and Migrations

TABLE 7

NETHERLANDS: NATURALIZATIONS ACCORDING TO COUNTRY OF FORMER NATIONALITY

	1988		1989	
	TOTAL	%	TOTAL	%
BELGIUM	110	1.2	250	0.9
FRANCE	30	0.3	100	0.3
GERMANY	270	3.0	670	2.3
GREECE	40	0.4	90	0.3
ITALY	90	1.0	150	0.5
PORTUGAL	70	0.8	220	0.8
SPAIN	50	0.5	100	0.3
UNITED KINGDOM	860	9.4	1 880	6.5
OTHER E.C.	20	0.2	30	0.1
TOTAL E.C.	1 540	16.9	3 490	12.1
TURKEY	820	9.0	3 280	11.4
YUGOSLAVIA	110	1.2	520	1.8
MOROCCO	1 190	13.1	6 830	23.8
SURINAM	830	9.1	3 570	12.4
OTHER	4 620	50.7	11 040	38.4
TOTAL	9 110	100.0	28 730	100.0

Source: (Dutch) Central Statistical office 1989/6

TABLE 8
UNITED KINGDOM: NATURALIZATIONS ACCORDING TO COUNTRY OF FORMER NATIONALITY

	1988		1989	
	Total	%	Total	%
EUROPEAN COMMUNITY	1 000	1.5	2 000	1.7
OTHER EUROPEAN	1 100	2.2	2 100	1.8
UNITED STATES	400	0.6	700	0.6
SOUTH AFRICA	1 800	2.8	2 700	2.3
PAKISTAN	4 800	7.4	7 500	6.4
FORMER COMMONWEALTH	1 200	1.9	3 500	3.0
NEW COMMONWEALTH	42 500	65.8	75 100	64.1
BRIT. CITIZENS OVERSEAS	3 000	4.6	5 000	4.3
OTHER	8 500	13.2	18 500	15.8
TOTAL	64 600	100.0	117 100	100.0

Source: Home Office ...ulletin, Citizenship Statistics, United Kingdom, 1989

TABLE 9
GERMANY: INFORMATION AVAILABLE ON ENTRIES OF FOREIGNERS (a)

	1983	1984	1985	1986	1987	1988	WOMEN ONLY	1989
BELGIUM	23.7	23.6	22.8	23.0	22.9	23.1	23.3	11.8
GREECE	10.0	9.3	9.5	11.8	15.5	33.0	13.0	
ITALY	35.7	37.5	38.9	46.1	45.0	41.8	15.4	
PORTUGAL	1.5	1.4	1.6	3.1	3.1	3.6	1.6	
SPAIN	2.8	3.1	3.2	4.1	3.8	3.9	2.0	
TURKEY	27.8	34.1	17.5	62.1	66.3	78.1	39.7	
YUGOSLAVIA	17.2	19.4	22.4	26.1	34.0	55.7	25.6	
MOROCCO	1.8	2.1	3.0	3.9	3.8	4.5	1.9	
TUNISIA	1.5	1.5	1.6	1.9	2.1	2.2	0.9	
OTHER	174.9	222.7	270.5	319.2	298.7	125.1	196.1	
TOTAL	273.2	331.1	398.2	478.3	472.3	648.5	296.2	770.8
women only	120.0	147.0	170.6	206.9	216.4	296.2		

(a) Entries recorded in municipal registers (including asylum-seekers) and collected in the central Registers of Foreigners

Source: Federal Statistical Office

TABLE 10

FRANCE: INFORMATION AVAILABLE ON ENTRIES OF FOREIGNERS (A)

	1983	1984	1985	1986	1987	1988	1989
ALGERIA	–	–	–	5.3	5.3	4.9	6.3
MOROCCO	15.3	11.4	9.0	8.2	8.6	10.8	13.6
POLAND	–	–	–	–	1.1	0.9	1.4
PORTUGAL	6.3	4.6	4.0	1.8	0.4	0.6	0.9
SPAIN	1.3	1.0	0.8	0.4	0.2	0.3	0.3
TUNISIA	5.3	3.4	2.5	2.4	2.6	2.9	3.2
TURKEY	6.8	5.4	4.3	4.3	4.6	4.7	5.3
YUGOSLAVIA	0.6	0.5	0.4	0.4	0.5	0.6	0.6
ASIA-PACIFIC		4.4	5.0	6.4			
OTHER	28.6	25.1	22.4	15.5	11.3	13.3	15.2
TOTAL	64.2	51.4	43.4	38.3	39.0	44.0	53.2

Figures correspond to new permanent foreign workers and foreigners joining their families, excluding EC residents –
workers and families – who have not been proposed. By the OMI as well as those seeking asylum.

Source: OMI (Office des migrations internationales).

TABLE 11

...RLANDS: INFORMATION AVAILABLE ON ENTRY OF FOREIGNERS(a)

	1983	1984	1985	1986	1987	1988	1989	women only
BELGIUM	1.6	1.5	1.9	2.3	2.4	2.3	2.2	1.0
FRANCE	0.9	1.2	1.1	1.4	1.5	1.6	1.6	0.7
GERMANY	4.2	4.2	4.1	4.3	4.1	4.4	4.6	2.3
ITALY	0.6	0.6	0.7	0.8	0.9	0.9	1.0	0.3
UNITED KINGDOM	3.5	3.8	4.0	4.4	4.5	4.0	4.2	1.7
OTHER E.C.	0.7	0.7	1.3	–	–	2.7	2.4	1.1
TOTAL E.C. (b)	11.5	12.0	13.1	–	–	15.9	16.0	7.1
POLAND	–	–	–	–	–	0.7	1.1	0.7
MOROCCO	4.9	4.8	5.8	6.6	7.0	8.2	8.4	3.5
SURINAM	3.0	1.7	3.2	3.7	4.3	2.9	4.4	2.5
TURKEY	3.7	4.1	5.9	8.4	9.6	10.4	11.0	4.5
UNITED STATES	1.9	2.0	2.3	2.0	2.0	2.0	2.3	1.1
ASIA	5.4	6.2	8.6	–	–	8.0	8.8	3.9
OTHER	6.0	6.5	7.3	18.9	24.6	10.2	13.4	5.4
TOTAL	36.4	37.3	46.2	52.8	60.9	58.3	65.4	28.7
women only	18.5	18.4	21.2	24.6	26.1	26.2	28.7	

(a) Figures correspond to foreign residents accounted for in municipal registers, including asylum-seekers.
(b) Total includes Spain, Portugal and Greece for every year recorded.
Source: (Dutch) Central Office of Statistics

TABLE 12
UNITED KINGDOM: INFORMATION AVAILABLE ON ENTRY OF FOREIGNERS(a)

	1984	1985	1986	1987	1988	1989
LONG-TERM TOTAL	6.8	7.1	7.9	8.1	10.4	13.3
INCLUDING						
WESTERN EUROPE	0.9	0.8	0.7	0.6	1.3	1.8
UNITED STATES	2.5	2.5	2.4	2.6	3.4	4.2
CANADA	0.3	0.2	0.3	0.3	0.4	0.4
AUSTRALIA-NEW ZEALAND	0.4	0.5	0.5	0.5	0.8	1.5
JAPAN	1.0	1.3	1.4	1.5	2.1	2.2
INDIA	0.2	0.3	0.3	0.3	0.5	0.6
HONG-KONG	0.4	0.4	0.3	0.3	0.5	0.7
SOUTH AFRICA	0.1	0.2	0.2	0.2	0.3	0.4
MALAYSIA	0.3	0.4	0.1	0.1	0.5	0.7
OTHER	0.7	0.5	1.7	1.7	0.6	0.8
SHORT-TERM TOTAL	6.2	6.6	8.0	9.4	11.8	12.2
TRAINEES TOTAL(b)	2.7	2.9	2.8	2.9	3.8	4.2
TOTAL	15.7	16.6	18.7	20.4	26.0	29.7

(a) Persons subject to immigration control must, in order to procure employment, obtain a permit issued by the Department of Employment overseas labour Division. There are three main categories for work permits: long-term, short-term, and those issued to trainees. In the majority of cases long-term permits are issued to those who are highly-qualified. Short-term permits also include students occupying temporary or part time posts and those whose university courses require them to undergo industrial placement, E.C countries are not included.
(b) Industrial Training programmes commonwealth citizens may be accepted in this category for several years, but for foreign students work experience may not exceed one year.
Source. Department of Employment (unpublished)

BIBLIOGRAPHY

Abanan-Unat, N., 1982, 'The effect of international labor migration on women's roles: the Turkish case', in C. Kagitcibasi, (ed.), *Sex Roles, Family, and Community in Turkey*, Bloomington, Indiana University Press, pp. 207–36.

Akhtar, S., 1989, *Be Careful with Muhammad*, London, Bellew Publishing.

Albrecht, G., 1972, *Soziologie des geographischen Mobilität. Zugleich ein Beitrag zur Soziologie des sozialen Wandels*, Stuttgart, Enke.

Anwar, M., 1979, *The Myth of Return: Pakistanis in Britain*.

Anwar, M., 1990, 'Asians in the British political system', in Clarke, Peach and Vertovec, p. 301.

Ball, W. and Solomos, J., 1990, *Race and Local Politics*, London, Macmillan.

Bolkestein, F. 1991, 'Integratie van minderheden moet met lef worden aangepakt', *De Volkskrant*, 12 september.

Borkowski, J.L., 1990, 'L'insertion sociale des immigrés et de leurs enfants', *Données sociales*, INSEE, pp. 310–314.

Brogan, D. and Kutner, N.G., 1976, 'Measuring sex-role orientations: a normative approach', *Journal of Marriage and the Family*, n° 38, pp. 31–40.

Clarke, C., Peach, C. and Vertovec, S., 1990, *South Asians Overseas: Migration and Ethnicity*, Cambridge, Cambridge University Press.

Delcroix, C. 1991, 'Politique d'intégration locale aux Pays-Bas', Didier Lapeyronnie (ed.), *Les politiques locales d'intégration des minorités immigrées en Europe et aux États-Unis*, Paris, ADRI, pp. 151–214.

Eade, J., 1990, 'Bangladeshi community organisation and leadership in Tower Hamlets, East London', Clarke, Peach and Vertovec, p. 301.

Eade, J., 1991, 'Changing landscapes in an "inner city" area: mosques, conservation and culture in Tower Hamlets', paper given to the conference on *Religions, Minorities and Social Change*, Bristol University, September 1991.

Entzinger H., 1985, 'The Netherlands', in Tomas Hammar (ed.), *European Immigration Policy*, Cambridge, Cambridge University Press, pp. 50–88.

Entzinger, H. and Carter, J., (eds), 1989, *Immigration in Western Democracies: The United States and Europe Compared*, Greenwich, Conn., JAI Press.

Entzinger, H.B. and Stijnen P.J.J. (eds.), 1990, *Etnische minderheden in Nederland*, Meppel-Heerlen, Boom-Open Universiteit.

Entzinger, H.B., 1994, 'De andere grenzen van de verzorgingsstaat', G. Engbersen, A. Hemerijck and W. Bakker (eds), *Zorg in het Europese huis: Grenzen van nationale verzorgingsstaten*, Amsterdam/Meppel, Boom.

Esser, H., 1980, *Aspekte der Wanderungssoziologie*, Darmstadt-Neurwied, Luchterhand.

Étienne, B., 1987, *L'Islamisme radical*, Paris, Hachette.

Francis, E.K., 1965, *Ethnos und Demos*, Berlin, 1965, *Interethnic Relations*, New York-Oxford-Amsterdam, 1976.

Gellner, E., 1983, *Nations and Nationalism*, Oxford.

Gerholm, T. and Lithman, Y.G., 1988, *The New Islamic Presence in Western Europe*, London, Mansell.

Gouldbourne, H., 1990, *Black Politics in Britain*, Aldershot, Avebury.

Haleber, R., ed., 1989, *Rushdie-Effekten*, Amsterdam, p. 147.

Hamidullah, M., 1941–1942, *Muslim Conduct of State*, Hyderabad, Government Central Press, pp. 68–75.

Harvey, L.P., 1964, 'Crypto-Islam in sixteenth century Spain', in *Actas del Primer Congreso de estudios arabes y islamicos*, Madrid, pp. 163–78.

Harvey, L.P., 1990, *Islamic Spain: 1250 to 1500*, Chicago, University Press, pp. 55–67.

Heckmann, F., 1992, *Ethnische Minderheiten, Volk und Nation Soziologie interethnischer Beziehungen*, Stuttgart.

Hill, P.B., 1984, *Determinanten der Eingliederung von Arbeitsmigranten*, Königstein.

Hirsch Ballin, E.M.H., 1988, *Overheid, Godsdienst en Levensovertuiging: Eindrapport criteria voor Steunverlening aan Kerkgenootschappen en andere genootschappen op Geestelijke Grondslag*, The Hague.

Hoffmann-Nowotny, H.J., 1970, *Migration*, Stuttgart, Enke.

Huber, B., 1987, 'Aktuelle Unzulänglichkeiten des Einbürgerungsrechts vor dem Hintergrund von Migrationsprozessen', in Barwig *et al.* (eds), *Aufenthalt-Niederlassung-Einbürgerung*, Baden-Baden.

Jeffery, P., 1976, *Migrants and Refugees: Muslim and Christian Pakistani Families in Bristol*, Cambridge, University Press.

Kagitcibasie, C., 1982, *The Changing Value of Children in Turkey*, Honolulu, East-West Center.

Kepel, G., 1987, *Les Banlieues de l'islam*, Le Seuil.

Khadduri, M., 1966. *The Islamic Law of Nations: Shybani's Siyar*,

Baltimore, MD, The Johns Hopkins Press, pp. 138–41, 187–94.

Khoury, A.T., 1985, *Islamische Minderheiten in der Diaspora*, Mainz, Grünewald, Kaiser.

Kimminich, O., 1985, *Rechtsprobleme der polyethnischen Staatsorganisation*, Munich Mainz.

König, P., Schultze, G. and Wessel, R., 1986, *Situation der ausländischen Arbeitnehmer und ihrer Familienangehörigen in der Bundesrepublik Deutschland*, Bonn, Bundesminster für Arbeit und Sozialordnung.

Lelohe, M., 1990, 'The Asian vote in a northern city', in H. Gouldbourne (ed.), *op. cit.*

Lenk, K., 1971, *Volk und Staat, Strukturwandel politischer Ideologien im 19 und 20 Jahrhundert*, Stuttgart-Berlin-Mainz-Cologne.

Lepsius, M.R., 1986, 'Ethnos und Demos', in *Kölner Zeitschrift für Soziologie und Sozialpsychologie*, pp. 751–9.

Leveau, R. and Kepel G. (eds), 1988, *Les Musulmans dans la société française*, Paris, Presses de la Fondation nationale des sciences politiques.

Lijphart, A., 1975, *The Politics of Accommodation: Pluralism and Democracy in the Netherlands*, Berkeley, University of California Press.

Linton, R., 1942, 'Nativistic movements', *American Anthropologist*, vol. 45, pp. 230–40.

Lucassen, J. and Penninx, R., 1985, *Nieuwkomers: Immigranten en hun nakomelingen in Nederland, 1550–1985*, Amsterdam, Meulenhoff.

Lucassen, L. and Köbben A.J.F., 1992, *Het partiële gelijk*, Leiden, COMT.

Masud, M.K., 1990, 'The obligation to migrate: the doctrine of Hijra in Islamic Law', in Dale F. Eickelman and James Piscatori (eds), *Muslim Travellers: Pilgrimage, Migration, and the Religious Imagination*, London, Routledge, pp. 29–49.

Meningen over Medelanders, 1992, *Meningen over ... Medelanders: 'Integratie of assimilatie'?*, Weert, M&P.

Minderhedennota, 1983, 's-Gravenhage, Ministerie van Binnenlandse Zaken.

Modood, T., 1990, *Muslims, Race and Equality in Britain*, Birmingham, Centre for the Study of Islam and Christian-Muslim Relations.

Muus, P.J., 1991, *Migration, Minorities and Policy in the Netherlands: Recent Trends and Developments* (SOPEMI Netherlands – 1991), University of Amsterdam, Centre for Migration Research.

Muxel, A., 1988, 'Les attitudes socio-politiques des jeunes issus de l'immigration maghrébine en région parisienne', *Revue française de sciences politiques*, n° 38, June 1988, pp. 925–39.

Nauck, B., 1988, 'Zwanzig Jahre Migrantenfamilien in der Bundesrepublik. Familiärer Wandel zwischen Situationsanpassung, Akkulturation und Segregation', in R. Nave-Herz (ed.), *Wandel und Kontinuität der Familie in der Bundesrepublik Deutschland*, Stuttgart, Enke, pp. 279–97.

Nauck, B., 1992, 'Ausländische Frauen in der Bundesrepublik Deutschland', in G. Helwig and H.M. Nickel, (eds), *Frauen in Deutschland*, Bonn, Bundeszentrale für politische Bildung.

Nederlands Centrum Buitenlanders, 1993, *Het jaar van de omslag; Inhoudelijk jaarverslag 1992*, Utrecht.

Nederlands Gesprek Centrum, 1992, 'De toekomstkansen van allochtone jongeren', Ministerie van Binnenlandse Zaken, *Maatschappelijk debat integratie*, 's-Gravenhage, pp. 15–76.

Nederlandse Dierenbescherming, 1984, *Slachten door middel van de Halssnede*, May, pp. 28, 39.

Ouseley, H., 1990, 'Resisting institutional change', in W. Ball, and J. Solomos, p. 135.

Penninx, R., Schoorl, J. and van Praag, C., 1993, *The Impact of International Migration on Receiving Countries: The Case of the Netherlands*, Amsterdam, Lisse, Swets & Zeitlinger.

Peters, R., 1979, *Islam and Colonialism: the Doctrine of Jihad in Modern History*, The Hagne, Mouton.

Rasoel, M., 1990, *De Ondergang van Nederland: Land der Naieve Dwazen*, Amsterdam, Gerard Timmer Prods, p. 116 *et seq.*

Rutten S., 1988, *Moslims in de Nederlanse Rechtspraak*, Kampen.

Sadan, J., 1980, '"Community" and "extra-community" as a legal and literary problem', in Joel L. Kraemer and Ilai Alon, *Religion and Government in the World of Islam*, Israel Oriental Studies, vol. X, Tel-Aviv, pp. 102–115.

Saïd, E.W., 1979, *Orientalism*, New York, Vintage Books.

Santillana, D., 1926, *Istituzioni di diritto musulmano malichita con riguardo anche al sistema sciafiita*, Rome, Anonima Romana Editoriale, vol. I, pp. 68–71, 75–6.

Sayad, A., 1991, *L'Immigration ou les Paradoxes de l'altérité*, Brussels, De Boeck-Westmael.

Schiedert, T., 1978, 'Typologie und Erscheinungsformen des Nationalismus', in H.A. Winkler (ed.), Nationalismus, Königstein.

Schnapper, D., 1989, '*La nation, les droits de la nationalité et L'Europe*, in *Revue Européenne des Migrations Internationales*, pp. 21–31.

Schnapper, D., 1991, *La France de l'intégration, Sociologie de la Nation en 1990*, Paris, Gallimard, 'Bibliothèque des sciences humaines'.

Schnapper, D., 1992, *L'Europe des immigrés, essai sur les politiques d'immigration*, Paris, François Bourin.

Schrader, A., Nikles, B.W. and Griese, H.M., 1979, *Die zweite Generation*, Königstein, 2. Aufl. Atenäum.

Shadid, W.A.R. and Van Koningsveld, P.S., 1990, *Moslims in Nederland*, Alphen aan de Rijn, p. 83; and same authors, 1989, in R. Haleber (ed), *Rushdie-Effekten*, Amsterdam, p. 133.

Shaw, A., 1989, *A Pakistani Community in Britain*, Oxford, University Press.

Sociaal en Cultureel Planbureau, 1992, *Sociale en Culturele Verkenningen 1992*, Rijswijk.

Tesser, P., 1993, *Rapportage minderheden 1993*, Rijswijk, Sociaal en Cultureel Planbureau.

Treibel, A., 1990, *Migration in modernen Gesellschaften. Soziale Folgen von Einwanderung und Gastarbeit*, Weinheim-Munich, Juventa.

Turki, A.M., 1980, 'Consultation juridique d'al-Imam al-Mazari sur le cas des Musulmans vivant en Sicile sous l'autorité des Normands', Beirut, Mélanges de l'université St. Joseph, vol. I, pp. 691–704.

Van den Bedem, R.F.A., 1993, *Motieven voor naturalisatie*, Arnhem, Gouda Quint.

Van Dugteren, F., 1993, *Woonsituatie minderheden*, Rijswijk, Sociaal en Cultureel Planbureau.

Wallmans, S., 1979, Foreword and Introduction to Wallman (ed.), 'Ethnicity at work', London.

Al-Wansharīsī, A., 1957, *Asnā al-matājir fī bayān ahkām man gha-laba 'ala waṭanihi al-Naṣārā wa-lam yuhājir*, Madrid, Husayn Mu'nis (ed.), *Revista des Instituto egipcio de estudios islamicosen Madrid*, p. 129–91.

Watt, W.M., 1991, *Muslim-Christian Encounters*, London, Routledge.

Wright, P., 1985, *On Living in an Old Country*, London, Verso.

Wrr (Scientific Council for Government Policy), 1979, *Ethnic Minorities*, The Hague.

Wrr (Scientific Council for Government Policy), 1989, *Immigrant Policy*, The Hague.

Zaal, W., 1991, *De Verlakkers*, Amsterdam, p. 174.